"I Want to Work in an Association—Now What??? is a terrific informational springboard for those new to the association world. It breaks down the essentials of what you truly need to know and will prepare you for the next steps—a foray into a deeply enriching and enjoyable field. Charlotte clearly has a passion for the industry and importantly, delivers the roadmap for others to pursue that passion for themselves."
Liz Giannini, Assistant Director, Membership Marketing, Association Forum of Chicagoland

"Just because we tumbled into the profession doesn't mean we shouldn't pursue our career methodically. As someone who wandered into an association by accident and only left the not-for-profit sector 25 years later to retire, I feel this book makes a major contribution and came only 20 years too late for me.

Just about everything you need to manage your career path through associations rather than letting it manage you is here in this book. Job search for that first and subsequent positions, promotions, marketing yourself, networking, and particularly personal branding are topics that I read closely and nodded with while I read. It's great to see an author within our sector capture so much of the good advice I've had to piece together through many searches and years of learning from colleagues in my jobs and volunteer positions, recruiters, and other resources."
Kevin Whorton, Former Vice Chair ASAE Marketing Section Council; Former Chair, Direct Marketing Association Non-Profit Federation; Former Executive, National Association of Home Builders, American Society of Health-System Pharmacists, National Association of Chain Drug Stores, and Catholic Relief Services

"Finally, a book provides an easy-to-understand contextual definition of what it is to work for an association! If only I'd had something like this when I was entering my first association job...maybe the learning curve would have been less steep. Kudos to the author who manages to convey the essence of the association world!"
KiKi L'Italien, Senior Consultant, Technology Management & Social Media Strategy, DelCor Technology Solutions

"It just shows this book is relevant whether you are a recent college graduate considering a career in associations, or a seasoned association professional. The resume tips and section on utilizing social media to leverage the career search were innovative and right on point. This book should be a mainstay in every college library and career counseling office."
Lindsey Lozmack, Executive Director, Association Development Solution

"What a fantastic resource! This book is a useful tool not only for those considering working for an association, but also for individuals, like myself, who have worked for associations for many years. I'll definitely keep this resource close at hand."
Deanna Menesses, CAE, Executive Director, Capital Area Medical Society

"True to its title, I Want to Work in an Association—Now What??? is a great resource for anyone who is considering a job or career in associations, but that is only the start. The hidden gem that this book possesses is that it is also a great resource for those who have not fully committed to the association world. Weeks does a great job illuminating the common and unique aspects of association life that make it an attractive option for job seekers. Furthermore, she provides excellent case studies and evidence-based advice— resources that serve as a great blueprint, which enables job seekers to be successful entering an association and advancing throughout their careers. The entire book is a true asset for the prospective association employee and a long overdue exposé for this sometimes misunderstood industry."
Demetrius Brown, Human Resources Generalist, American Dietetic Association

"I Want to Work in an Association—Now What??? is a great resource that I plan to give to each of my protégés. I found Chapter 5, 'Why Is Networking Important to My Association Career?' and Chapter 6, 'How Can Social Media Help My Job Search?' to be relevant, timely, and the perfect reference book that should be read by all rising executives!"
Stephen Peeler, Vice President of Membership, American Moving and Storage Association

I Want to Work in an Association— Now What???

A Guide to Getting a Job in a Professional Association, Membership Organization, or Society

By Charlotte Weeks, CCMC, NCRW, CPRW
Foreword by Sheri Jacobs, CAE

20660 Stevens Creek Blvd., Suite 210
Cupertino, CA 95014

Copyright © 2011 by Charlotte Weeks

Published by Happy About®
20660 Stevens Creek Blvd., Suite 210, Cupertino, CA 95014
http://happyabout.com

First Printing: August 2011
Paperback ISBN: 978-1-60005-195-1 (1-60005-195-2)
eBook ISBN: 978-1-60005-196-8 (1-60005-196-0)
Place of Publication: Silicon Valley, California, USA
Paperback Library of Congress Number: 2011933623

Trademarks

Warning and Disclaimer

Dedication

To Mike, the world's best husband, for his unconditional support and love.

To my grandma, Jane "Adams" Kucharski, who always loved to write.

Acknowledgments

There are so many people I want to thank for their part in putting this book together that I must apologize in advance if I leave anyone out.

First and foremost, a big thank you to the many people who contributed, whether by offering their views and experiences, providing a testimonial, or reviewing an early draft. Your insights give a depth to this book that would not have been possible otherwise.

I'd also like to thank the people who facilitated introductions with association professionals including: Jason Alba, Melissa Arthur, Nicholas Bailey, Liz Cies, Sima Dahl, Laura DeCarlo, Liz Giannini, J. Mori Johnson, Melanie Kaneas, Russ Kovar, Paul Rotatori, Mick Weltman, and Travis Wilson. I'd also like to express my gratitude to the staff at the Association Forum of Chicagoland, for patiently answering all of my many questions.

Next, I'd like to thank my business coach Susan Whitcomb for her sound advice and encouragement on the monumental task of writing a book! I'd also like to thank Robyn Feldberg for her early confidence when she nominated me to become the President of The National Resume Writers' Association.

Of course, this book would not have been possible without the staff at Happy About Publishing: Jason Alba, Mitchell Levy, Janae Pierre, Liz Tadman, and their editors—I am grateful to you all for your support, encouragement, and guidance!

And last but definitely not least, my husband and fellow author Mike Weeks. Thank you for all of your encouragement. I love you.

A Message From Happy About®

Thank you for your purchase of this Happy About book. It is available online at http://happyabout.com/workinassociation.php or at other online and physical bookstores.

- Please contact us for quantity discounts at sales@happyabout.info
- If you want to be informed by email of upcoming Happy About® books, please email bookupdate@happyabout.info

Happy About is interested in you if you are an author who would like to submit a non-fiction book proposal or a corporation that would like to have a book written for you. Please contact us by email editorial@happyabout.info or phone (1-408-257-3000).

Other Happy About books available include:

- I'm in a Job Search—Now What???:
  http://www.happyabout.com/jobsearchnowwhat.php
- Fast Track Guide to a Professional Job Search:
  http://www.happyabout.com/fasttrackjobsearch.php
- 42 Rules to Jumpstart Your Professional Success :
  http://bit.ly/42RulesJumpstart[1]
- I'm at a Networking Event—Now What???:
  http://www.happyabout.com/networking-event.php
- #JOBSEARCHtweet Book01:
  http://www.happyabout.com/thinkaha/jobsearchtweet01.php
- Happy About My Resume:
  http://www.happyabout.com/myresume.php
- Happy About The Career Alphabet:
  http://www.happyabout.com/happyaboutcareeralphabet.php
- The Successful Introvert
  http://www.happyabout.com/thesuccessfulintrovert.php
- I'm on LinkedIn—Now What???:
  http://www.happyabout.com/linkedinhelp.php
- iPad Means Business:
  http://www.happyabout.com/ipadmeansbusiness.php
- Storytelling about Your Brand Online & Offline:
  http://www.happyabout.com/storytelling.php
- Social Media Success!:
  http://www.happyabout.com/social-media-success.php

---

1. www.happyabout.com/42rules/jumpstartprofessionalservices.php

Contents

Contents

Foreword by Sheri Jacobs, CAE

Do you remember what you wanted to be when you grew up? If you were asked to think back to when you were in grade school, you might have responded by saying, "I want to be a vet, a teacher, or a professional baseball player." Most likely, you did not say, "I want to be an association professional."

When we were young we dreamt of pursuing our passions and helping others. We dreamed of traveling to far-off places and exploring new worlds. Our vision of what this may entail was based on our beliefs that anything and everything was possible—if you worked hard. Yet, our vision was also limited by what we saw on TV or our interactions with adults in our lives.

The one common trait among the answers given by children in response to the question, "What do you want to be when you grow up" is the feeling of pursuing something that is enjoyable and meaningful.

Although the association profession meets or exceeds all of these objectives, it is an accidental profession. In a random (and unscientific) survey of my colleagues, 100 percent stated they found their way to this profession by chance after working in corporate America or in another field altogether. Why is this the case? Because they lacked awareness of the opportunities and a roadmap for navigating the community.

Charlotte Weeks provides the association community, and the next generation of young professionals, an invaluable tool for finding a position that will be more than just a job. From "How-to" tips and suggestions to case studies and sample resumes, Weeks gives the reader an insider's look into how to find a fulfilling career in association management.

As you turn the pages, you will read first-hand accounts of how some association professionals have turned a chance encounter into a lifelong career. When you finish the book, I hope you will be inspired like I was to recommend this book to others who wish to find not just a job but also a meaningful career.

Sheri Jacobs, CAE
President + Chief Strategist
Avenue M Group
Author, *199 Ideas: Powerful Marketing Tactics That Sell* (ASAE 2010) and *Membership Essentials: Recruitment, Retention, Roles, Responsibilities, and Resources* (ASAE 2007)

Introduction

If career coaching and resume writing weren't my true passions, I would have been content to spend the rest of my career working in an association. Like many people, I fell into working for one (in human resources), and was immediately struck by how good a fit it was for me. Helping people was a high priority, but my previous experience in a nonprofit was not a good one. It was so small and low-budget that I did not have Internet access, and my desk wasn't even a desk, but a table! My pay was barely enough to live on, and there wasn't much room for growth. I figured I'd need to just get a corporate job and volunteer after hours if I wanted to help people.

Unexpectedly, I found out about associations. While they are still nonprofits, they fall into a class of their own. Associations are typically comprised of members (and employees) focused on furthering a specific profession. However, it goes much further than that. For example, healthcare organizations support professionals working in the industry, but they also educate the public on medical issues. They can also contribute to society by offering their unique skills during a time of crisis (for example, sending physicians, nurses, or paramedics to an earthquake-ravaged area).

Associations are often run like corporations, with the competitive pay and benefits that come with a corporation, but they are usually much more focused on the mission than on the bottom line. As in any organization, finances are important, but the needs of the members are a higher priority. In fact, when interviewing people for this book, I found that the most common answer to the question, "What do you think is most important to be aware of when applying for association positions?" was an awareness of being member-focused.

While I grew to feel passionate about the mission of the association I worked for (I initially didn't know much about the area), there are so many to choose from. Nearly every profession has at least one that represents the people in that field, and there are those that serve every facet of daily life. According to the Association FAQ page on the website of The American Society of Association Executives', The Center for Association Leadership (ASAE), in 2009 there were 90,908 trade and professional associations, and 1,238,201 philanthropic and charitable organizations.

Ironically, most of the people I interviewed for this book did not choose to work in an association, but instead "fell into" it. The answers to "how" varied widely. A few temped in college, some volunteered first (even as early as high school), and others just applied to an association along with many other types of organizations. Regardless of how they got there, all ended up enjoying associations immensely.

Whether you want to break into the association industry or are a seasoned professional, this book will help you find your next opportunity!

About This Book

The information in *I Want to Work in an Association—Now What???* comes from a variety of sources. I drew on my experiences of working in the human resources department of an association and leading The National Resume Writers' Association, along with the knowledge I've gained in my career as a career coach and resume writer.

My research also included reviewing content found in numerous association periodicals, websites, and newsletters, and attending industry seminars and workshops. Of course, the single greatest source of information came from the more than 50 association professionals that shared their experiences with me. Ranging from entry-level employees to CEOs, from career changers to "lifers," and running the gamut across job function and association industry, each shared valuable insights with me and many are quoted here.

"*I completely fell into association work. I started working as a temp during college at the American Subcontractors Association. The association had two summer meetings, so they always needed help in the summer. It got to the point that ASA called me at school to find out when I'd be home in the summer to work. Once I finished school, I was working part-time for ASA and substitute teaching. A full-time position opened up in the government relations department and I decided that I needed the benefits and could always go back to teaching. Almost 25 years later, I'm still in the industry.*"
Karin Soyster Fitzgerald, CMP, CAE, Vice President, Membership Services, American Bakers Association

DISCLAIMER: *Please note that opinions expressed by individuals do not necessarily reflect those of their employers.*

1 Why Would You Want to Work in an Association?

Contrary to popular belief, nonprofits and associations are not interchangeable. While it's true that associations are nonprofits, there are major differences between them.

According to the IRS, the definition of an association can vary by state. However, they also say "in general, an association is a group of persons banded together for a specific purpose." The term society is used interchangeably with association, and the common thread between all is membership. Every association includes people who join to further a common interest.

There are various types of associations, but this book will primarily focus on two categories. Professional associations are those made up of individuals dedicated to a specific profession (such as the National Association of Realtors), and trade associations, which consist of business owners promoting their industry (such as the Newspaper Association of America).

What Do Associations Do?

In general, education, awareness, and advocacy are at the heart of many organizations. Since most of them focus on furthering a profession, it benefits them to make sure their members are trained and representing the industry well. Not only are the members on the cutting-edge, they are also the thought leaders who grow the profession. This keeps the industry relevant, which means more opportunities for the members and more value to their customers.

The certification that many associations offer is often the most visible result of education. Members typically have to meet certain requirements (such as being in the profession for a minimum number of years) before they can even sit for a certification exam. Once they have passed, they usually need to obtain continuing education units to maintain the credential. This process not only ensures that the members of the profession are kept up to date, it also assures the public that these individuals are established in their industry. These credentials set a standard of knowledge and also create loyalty, both to the profession and the industry.

Many organizations are affected by government decisions (for example, medical and environmental legislation will inevitably impact associations that focus on those issues). If members of a profession want to advocate for a change in policy, they will have more impact as an association than if they were to each go it alone.

At the heart of everything, associations focus on providing members with whatever is of most value to them. According to Nicholas Bailey, Workforce Development Manager, Association Forum of Chicagoland, "associations run like a for-profit, except that all additional income goes back to the organization and its members."

Why Are They Good Employers?

One thing that makes associations appealing is the fact that the salary is not that far off from that offered by for-profit corporations. Of course this can vary greatly by association and position, but many of the people I interviewed for this book found this to be the case in their own experience. Considering that a common reason that people avoid nonprofit work is the belief that they would have to choose between making a good living or making a difference, it's encouraging to know that in an association, the two are not mutually exclusive.

How is this possible, when an association is still a nonprofit? The difference is that the focus of a corporation is the bottom-line, and the focus of an association is the needs of the members, the organization, and the industry. Simply put, people come first. This is illustrated by the fact that according to the Association Forum of Chicagoland's "2010–2011 Compensation and Benefits Survey," many associations have increased the availability of alternative benefits such as tuition reimbursement, flextime scheduling, and telecommuting.

Another great thing about working in an association is that there are so many opportunities. In some ways, it's a "hot" area. In fact, according a March article in CEO Update, new association job listings are up by more than an astonishing 45 percent in the first two months of 2011! In addition, there are associations throughout the U.S., with the highest concentration found in Washington, D.C.

If you're sold on targeting associations, the job type is almost secondary. Whatever your field in a corporate job, chances are there's a comparable position in an association. Most have finance, human resources (HR), information technology (IT), and marketing departments, plus there are association-specific areas such as membership and fundraising (where you may be able to apply transferable skills, such as sales). In addition, associations usually have departments that focus on the industry being served. For example, many medical associations have doctors on staff conducting research, writing for a medical journal, or advising marketing on how to appeal to potential physician members.

Of course, associations face some of the same downsides as other industries. They still have layoffs, some don't provide much room for advancement, and red tape and politics are still a factor. Like anything else, these risks can vary greatly by each organization and should be carefully considered when applying to a particular association.

Changing the World

Being able to make a difference in the world is a major motivator for association employees. Some knew before they even started their careers that helping people was a must-have aspect of whatever job they held. Others found this out after they "fell into" association work, and now wouldn't have it any other way. According to Melissa Arthur, a former Peace Corps volunteer, "association work is the perfect blend of the nonprofit and for-profit worlds." Melissa has found that she could still contribute to a mission important to her, and still be able to make a good living. Now the Manager of Chapter Services at the Institute of Real Estate Management, she says, "We are not dependent upon governmental grants or philanthropic support. We are funded by our members and have a number of resources at our disposal." Organizations funded in this manner are less likely to have the financial upheavals that corporate and philanthropic places have.

Others are unified by a common cause. Whether it's a mission for which they have always been passionate or have grown to care about, many employees are motivated to see their industries expand. As president of The National Resume Writers' Association, I have been amazed by the willingness of our members to volunteer their time and talent. Though this organization is driven by volunteers, many contribute out of desire to promote recognition of our industry, help their colleagues, and raise standards—and I have observed the same passion in association employees. According to Scott Oser, Sales, Marketing, Membership and Circulation Consultant with Scott Oser Associates, Inc., "Associations are created around a need and they provide benefits to members and consumers that fulfill that need. The association community is very open, inviting and inclusive. After working in the association world for fifteen years, I have met some incredible people that I go out of my way for and they will do the same for me. I actually was not really involved in the association industry for a number of years and when I returned I reconnected quickly and easily with many people I had relationships with prior to my disappearance."

Conclusion

Associations offer "something for everyone" whether employees, members, or the general public. Many associations indirectly help with employment, by offering educational and networking opportunities to their members. At the same time, they are helping the recipients of the members' services by training them on the latest industry trends. Regardless of the mission, each is founded to benefit the greater good.

So you know you want to work for an association. Now what?

What others have said about why they enjoy working in the association industry:

"Members, mission, and camaraderie. Members are the best-committed to their clients and to improving their profession. And the associations I have worked for have been filled with very bright, very committed staff members. Even pulling together for a tote bag stuffing can be fun."
Janet McEwan, Director, Corporate Relations, American Society of Radiologic Technologists.

"I find association jobs to be filled with purpose. The work is often done by very passionate people."
Becky Rice, former Director of Marketing, American Immigration Lawyers Association

"Since I was a member, I feel I am furthering the profession."
Shayne Kavanagh, Senior Manager-Research, Government Finance Officers Association

"It just isn't on the radar of people just entering the work-world. It's the best profession that no one knows about!"
Patricia Leeman, CAE Principal, Leeman Consulting Services, LLC

What's an association management company (AMC)?

These for-profit companies provide the services that associations require to function: administrative, financial, membership development, etc. They often work for multiple organizations that don't have the need or resources for a full-time staff. This ends up being a cost-effective solution for small, all-volunteer, or start-up organizations.

"As with most for-profit companies, an AMC's direction comes from the CEO as opposed to a Board of Directors, where there is a propensity to have multiple and changing directives."
Randall Van Den Berghe, Senior Director, Human Resources, CMI

2 What Type of Association and Job Do You Want?

If "any type" is your answer, think again. Job searches are *much* more effective when there is a clear goal. As the saying goes, "if you don't know where you're going, how will you get there?" You don't need to have such a narrow focus that you limit yourself to just one or two organizations (in fact, you shouldn't—the job search is often a numbers game, and the more places you look, the higher your odds). However, you should definitely know the area, function, and level you're seeking (e.g. marketing division, director-level), and it can be helpful to target associations that specialize in an area you're passionate about.

So how do you figure out what to do "when you grow up?" While some people figure this out gradually over the course of their career, a self-reflective process analyzing what you want (and don't want) can help you get to this point more quickly. Keep in mind, this is more than just interests. Things such as your skills, financial requirements, desired geographic location, and the state of the market all need to be taken into account. While no job is perfect, once you identify what's a deal-breaker and what would be "gravy," you'll be able to narrow down the options even further. Only you can know what's best for you, but the guidelines and questions below will help get you thinking. The case study at the end of each category illustrates how a person's answers can bring them closer to identifying what they want in a job.

Skills: What have you been "known for" on and off the job? Which tasks come easily to you? In which areas have you had the most success? Don't limit yourself to skills you've used on the job. Consider hobbies, volunteer work, or even things that you were good at while you were in school. At this point, don't worry about how your expertise will fit into a job.

Case Study: Grace is the "go-to person" for all client presentations. In college, she performed in plays, frequently in a leading role. One of her hobbies is singing. Clearly, Grace could be considered for roles that involve public speaking (one possibility: in-house trainer).

Interests: What do you do in your free time? What are the topics of most of the books you read? What type of volunteer work do you like to do? When you were a kid what did you want to be "when you grew up?" What have been your favorite duties throughout your career? Answers to all of these questions can give you insights on both what job functions and which industries you'd enjoy.

Case Study: After work, William takes classes to learn French. Growing up, he wanted to be a pilot. He's never shied away from business travel, and enjoys meeting people and learning about other cultures. A job with heavy travel may be the ticket for William. With his love of people and new places, a potential job could be a liaison between U.S. and international branches.

Finances: If you find your dream job, but it doesn't pay you enough to keep a roof over your head, it really isn't the right position for you. Still, though salary is likely an important factor in any job, it is only part of the equation. The benefits package, which typically includes health insurance, retirement plans, and vacation days, also needs to be considered. Before beginning your job search, determine exactly how much you need to make and which benefits are must-haves.

Case Study: Harry would like to be paid well, but more important than that are the benefits an organization can provide. His wife makes a very good income at her job, but the health benefits leave a lot to be desired. Fortunately, she gets an entire month of vacation each year, and both she and Harry love to travel. Therefore, he will focus on acquiring a generous vacation allowance and quality health insurance, even if it means sacrificing pay.

Environment: Do you prefer to be in an office building five days a week? If so, is an office a must-have or is a cubicle fine? Would you rather be "out in the field" calling on clients? Do you want to have a structured 9 to 5 schedule, or would you prefer to have more flexibility (even if it means evenings and weekends)? Since 25 percent of your life is spent on the job, it's important that you are happy with your environment.

Case Study: Phillip doesn't really mind going into an office each day, as long as he doesn't need to keep rigid times. Eight or even ten hours a day is fine, as long as he can occasionally schedule doctor's appointments during the day or come in early and leave early when his kids have a soccer game. With these preferences, Phillip will ideally work in a company that provides flex-time, or at the very least, a laid-back culture.

Market: How is the job market for the type of work you're seeking? Does your dream association support a profession that's thriving? Have there been layoffs recently? Look five to ten years into the future. Where do the trends point?

Case Study: Caroline had been working for an association focused on the construction industry. She was hired at the height of a building boom, and despite a recession has been promoted several times. Whenever she hears about the organization losing members or another construction layoff, she wonders if she should look for a new job. The problem is, she really likes the industry and has built up a strong reputation. After conducting research on trends and projections, she decides to stay put. Though things are not great now, she feels confident that construction will rebound as the economy improves.

Which associations are the most secure? According to Jack McInerney, Chief Digital Officer of InTime TV, a video channel for associations, any organization that certifies its members is more likely be a stable employer. Jack also says that healthcare and engineering associations are less likely to have layoffs.

Create a List of Potential Job Functions and Associations

Using the information you've gathered above, write down all the possible jobs and organizations that come to mind. If you're unsure about what job functions are available, visit http://www.onetonline.org. Created for the U.S. Department of Labor, this helpful site has tools to help you identify occupations. It also provides you with detailed information on what you can expect from each role (including duties, salary, and outlook).

If it's associations you need more assistance with, visit http://www.weddles.com. Its association directory has links to thousands of organizations, all grouped by industry (e.g. fashion, telecommunications, travel, etc.). Use this resource to brainstorm industries and learn about specific associations at the same time.

Test the Options

Once you've narrowed down your functions/industries to a manageable number, it's time to conduct primary research. While this can take significant time, it's better to find out what you *don't* want now, rather than after you've started a new job. There are countless ways to explore an industry or organization, but the methods below are some of the most effective.

Volunteer

Not only can volunteering double as networking (see Chapter 5 to learn more about how to network and why it's important), but it can also help you find out whether or not an association is the right fit. If there's a cause you're passionate about, volunteering for organizations with the same focus could give you more of an "inside" view than you'd get from an interview. Whichever way you participate, you'll naturally meet members and employees.

Carly Caminiti, Manager, Mission Services, Tobacco Control and Community Outreach at the American Lung Association in Illinois, actually started her association career as a volunteer for the ALA—in high school! At an early age, she was able to confirm what she wanted to do for a living.

Not only can volunteering help you determine what type of industry you want to work in, it can also help you try out new tasks. If you've always worked in finance and are wondering about transitioning to marketing, offer to serve on an organization's marketing committee. You'll find out if you really do want to make the move, and you'll pick up new skills in the meantime.

Internship

Many people have had college internships where they learned exactly what areas they did *not* want to work in. Others have ended up with offers, and are still happily employed today. Either way, internships are a great way to try out careers, and they aren't just for college students!

People of all ages try for internships if they're interested in changing careers. Cindy Simpson, CAE, Director of Programs and External Relations, Association for Women in Science, recommends them as a way to both get your foot in the door and to learn more about a particular organization. To find opportunities, she says, "Internships may be found at many associations, and information would be available on the association's website. Set up times to meet with various people who are already in the association industry to talk with them about career opportunities."

Temping

Being a temporary employee for an association has multiple benefits. Not only are you getting paid, but you're also networking internally, and are probably getting access to posted jobs before anyone else. Even better, you get to "test drive" an organization, something that not everyone gets to do. Since employment agencies benefit from their temps staying on long term, they're usually very open to any feedback you have. If you truly dislike working somewhere, the agency can often assign you somewhere else. Hopefully, that situation is the exception to the rule, but regardless, you can see how you feel about an organization (and position, if you're temping in the one you hope to be hired into) before throwing your hat into the ring.

J. Mori Johnson, Director, International Medical Graduates Services and minority affairs, American Medical Association, found that temping for six months was a huge boost to her career. Coming from a different industry, she was able to learn how the association world worked. This "trial period" also gave her the opportunity to prove herself, and her employer ultimately ended up creating a new position for her.

Informational Interview

Informational interviews are one of the best ways to find out the "real deal" about a career before pursuing it. All the online research in the world can't compare to meeting face-to-face with someone in the trenches.

Like a regular job interview, it helps to have a warm lead. Identify people you know who work in your target area (this can often be accomplished through LinkedIn) and simply ask for help. Sonia Pagonakis, a job seeker who has worked as a program planner in associations, asked a friend to make an introduction to her "target," which ultimately led to an in-person informational interview.

If you just can't find anyone, a cold call is an option. Find out who you'd like to meet with by doing a search on LinkedIn or Twitter and contact them directly. It's less effective than an introduction, but when you approach it from an educational standpoint as opposed to a job search, you're more likely to get results.

When making initial contact, be clear about your expectations. State exactly how long you'd like to meet with the interviewee (remember, you're the one initiating the interview) and what it is you'd like to discuss. Then, stick to it! If you both agreed to fifteen minutes, and the conversation doesn't seem to be winding down, say something like, "I want to be respectful of your time, and I know our fifteen minutes is up. Would you like to end now or continue our discussion?" To stay on topic, come prepared with a list of questions. The person you're interviewing may offer more than you could have expected, but they'll appreciate the fact that you're focused, and also aren't expecting a job offer. Whatever you do, don't offer your resume (which immediately implies that all along your agenda has been a job, not an informational interview). Only provide if asked.

What questions should you ask? Whatever it is you want to know. If you're considering an association with a different focus than those you've been in, a few ideas to get you started include:

1. What do you feel are some of the biggest challenges faced when working for an association focused on the XYZ profession?
2. How has this type of association furthered the XYZ industry, profession, etc.?
3. Where do you see XYZ and/or the XYZ association headed in the next five to ten years?
4. What are the qualifications required for someone starting out in a XYZ position?
5. What do you like about being a XYZ? What do you find more of a challenge?

Many of the same rules apply when following up after a traditional interview. Send a thank you letter immediately, or even consider sending a small token of your appreciation. Also, stay in touch through occasional e-mails or connecting on LinkedIn. Though the primary purpose of an informational interview is to learn, you also may make some valuable networking contacts.

Online Research

This is the easy one! Start with the basics, and check out the sites of several associations in your target industry. The "About Us" page can be especially helpful. After that, dig a little deeper by doing a Google search and go through a few pages. This is where you're more likely to find third-party opinions on an organization. Check out groups on LinkedIn or trending topics on Twitter to see what others are saying.

Once you've gotten a good grasp on your areas of interest, weigh the pros and cons (especially the deal breakers!). Cover as many topics as possible, using the categories early in this chapter as a guide. Think about the day to day routine, growth opportunities, salary, commute—anything that you feel is important to consider.

When it comes to researching a type of job, you can visit http://www.onetonline.com (described earlier in this chapter), or http://www.bls.gov/oco. The latter is the Occupational Outlook Handout, which profiles hundreds of jobs. Updated annually, it provides information on a profession's outlook, requirements, and salary.

Making a Decision

After all of this self-reflection and research, you still probably haven't found "the one" perfect job. That's because it doesn't exist. There are likely several jobs out there that would be a fit for you.

It's not easy, but to move forward you must make decisions so that you can conduct an effective job search. Look at your top few choices and consider the pros and cons of each. Consider which factors are deal breakers and must-haves, but also listen to your gut. While no job is perfect, don't ignore what your instincts are telling you!

3 Personal Branding for the Association Professional

What IS Personal Branding?

First of all, what *is* a brand? According to dictionary.com, it's defined as "kind, grade, or make, as indicated by a stamp, trademark, or the like." In a nutshell, a personal brand is how people remember you. Companies and celebrities—who are often companies in themselves—spend a lot of time developing and establishing a brand. More than just any one piece, the visible parts of a brand can include a slogan, color, or even just personal attributes. For example:

1. When you think of the color *orange*, which home improvement store comes to mind?
   a. Lowe's
   b. Home Depot
   c. Ace Hardware
2. Think of a very *generous* talk show host. Who comes to mind?
   a. Barbara Walters
   b. Phil Donahue
   c. Oprah Winfrey

3. What restaurant do you think of when you hear *"I'm Lovin' It?"*

   a. McDonald's
   b. Pizza Hut
   c. Subway

At least one, if not all, of these answers probably came to you easily, but here are the results: 1) b, 2) c, 3) a. Note that each of these companies and people have an easily identifiable *something*, even though the second one is completely intangible. Still, most of the public recognizes them in an instant, the result of both repeated and consistent messaging.

Why Is It Important to Have a Brand?

More than anything, brands help build trust, which inspires people to buy. Think about it. There are countless hamburger restaurants in the world, but McDonald's sells the most by a long shot. It's not that they're necessarily the best, but they've built a strong brand that communicates exactly what they provide—hamburgers served up fast and at a low price. People immediately recognize these advantages, and because of the organization's credibility and consistency, they are more comfortable buying from them.

You may see how this makes sense for a company, but not for an individual. Actually, there aren't that many differences outside of the size. Like a company does with potential customers, you are hoping to convince an employer to buy (hire you) by showing them why you're the best person for the job. These days, there are numerous channels that an association can use to learn about you. This is a good thing—as in marketing, the more your message gets across, the more likely it is that you'll be remembered. If your message is inconsistent, you're reducing the chances of being remembered. With intense competition for each open job, it helps to use every possible advantage!

Having a strong brand isn't just for job seekers. Using the McDonald's example again, why do you think they're still advertising? Because they need to stay top of mind and remind people of their advantages. The same applies to individuals throughout their career. You'll be more likely to be contacted by recruiters or recommended by colleagues if you have established a strong reputation. In addition, if you build your brand with an eye to the future, it can be helpful in your climb up the association ladder.

Why People Resist

Establishing a brand and then announcing it to the world can seem scary. It's easy to see why, since it's a commitment. The problem is that most people worry about becoming pigeonholed—they're concerned that they'll never be able to try anything new.

There are two reasons why this shouldn't be a concern. First, your brand should be something about you which will never change. For example, I know someone who has a reputation for knowing *everyone*. His core brand attribute is that he's a networker—something that will serve him no matter what his career. Of course, this is just one aspect of his character, and this brand should be tied in with how it can add value to an organization.

The other thing to keep in mind is that brands evolve. You've probably heard of the term "rebranding." It's something every company—and individual—will have to do at some point to stay viable.

So, rest assured, if you spend the time to create a strong brand, it will work for you at any point in your career.

How to Develop and Communicate YOUR Own Personal Brand

According to Sima Dahl, president of Sway Factor and an expert in social networking, your personal brand is equal parts character, competence, and charisma. "It's who you are, what you do, and why you're special," says Sima, adding, "It's your responsibility to create it, own it, and then make sure everyone knows what it is."

Developing the right brand for you can take time. Even when you do establish one that works for you, it may evolve throughout your career. Use the "what, how, and where" method to start building your brand, and then set it down for awhile. Come back later and tweak it until you feel it authentically communicates the advantages you can offer an employer.

The What

What do you want to be known for? What unique combination of qualities do you possess that could add value to an organization? How do other people describe you?

What you *want* to do should be considered just as much as what you have to offer. If you develop a reputation for something you don't like doing, you could end up trapped in a career you don't enjoy!

The How

Once you know *what* you want to be known for, you need to figure out *how* to communicate it. There are countless ways, but two necessities include a short branding message and the elevator pitch. These serve as a foundation for communicating through writing and through conversation. A branding message can be in different forms and can be included throughout all of your written materials—from your resume to your LinkedIn profile to your e-mail signature and your business cards. Anywhere people will "see" your brand, your tagline should be included. For example, here are two of the formats I use for my personal brand message:

Helping Association Executives Find Their Passion and Land at the Top! The longer of the two, I might use this in a LinkedIn profile or in the Facebook "about me" box.

Find Your Passion. Land at the Top. This version is short and to the point. It's ideal for Twitter, business cards, and e-mail signatures.

Clearly, the two items in my message fit the coaching industry. But deeper than that, it's about the core of what I offer. I'm passionate about motivating people to be their best selves, so this would apply to me regardless of my career. For example, even if I was the manager of a store (utilizing each employee's strengths to help them succeed on the job) or an administrative assistant (supporting my boss so she can do her job well), my brand still fits what I do.

The elevator pitch is what you'll typically say to people when you first meet them. With only about thirty seconds to capture attention *and* communicate your unique value proposition, it can be a challenge to create. Components include your name, what you do, what's unique about you, and what you're looking for. For example:

Sample Elevator Pitch

My name is Lily Landphere and I'm a human resources representative specializing in recruitment. I help associations improve retention to keep costs down. My last two employers were able to reduce turnover based on procedures I implemented during the hiring process. I'm looking to talk to decision makers in healthcare associations.

Keep in mind that your elevator pitch shouldn't sound rehearsed. Practice it over and over until it's second nature. Also, it won't be necessary to repeat this verbatim every time. Getting familiar enough with the basic pitch will make it easier for you to switch around as needed.

There are numerous subtle ways to communicate your brand, and it's often more art than science. The key is to be consistent. While you shouldn't necessarily use the exact same wording across every channel, it's important to bring the same message across each time.

The Where

The where usually includes platforms you're already using, but there are no limits to what you can use. Here is a partial list of suggestions as to where to incorporate your branding:

1. **Resume and Cover Letter:** Include your branding message at the top of both documents, just below the heading and job title. Then, back up your claims with examples in the body of each document.

2. **LinkedIn Profile:** Use your headline to show what you can do (these are likely to be keyword search terms) and save your branding statement for the first part of the summary. As in the resume, back up the statement with examples.

3. **Business Cards:** Choose a color, font, and design that "fit" you. Use these same stylistic elements in your other materials. Include your branding message, too.

4. **Social Media Sites:** Each site allows you to do different things, but in general, your written branding message should come across at some point. On Twitter, you can include it in your 160-character bio, and can have a custom-made background with your colors and style elements. For Facebook, the "about me" box (under your picture) should include your marketing message. For both sites (as well as LinkedIn), further establish your brand by posting statuses that tie back to your industry.

5. **Blog:** A blog is a *great* way to establish yourself as a subject matter expert. Include your branding message near the top, keep the colors in line with the rest of your materials, and keep your posts relevant to the topic you want to become known for.

6. **Personal Website:** A website can be developed similar to a blog (as far as the branding message and colors). For the rest of it, you can make it be whatever you want! Some ideas include articles you've written, a section on industry events, and links to news items about you.

7. **E-mail Signature:** You can use the same marketing message as your resume, cover letter, and business cards.

8. **Elevator Pitch:** This can be used when meeting someone for the first time. It's an ideal answer to the question, "what do you do?" —especially at a networking event.

It can take time and energy not only to develop your perfect brand, but also to communicate it consistently. Still, it's worth the effort. It will help you both during the job search and throughout your career.

How has personal branding made a difference in your career?

"Early in my career, I became known for certain skill sets. I further defined that brand by going through past performance reviews to see what statements people used to describe me. This helped me form my talking points—I decided in advance what I wanted people to remember about me."
Linda Woody, Communications Manager, Association Headquarters, Inc.

"I tried to think of my core strengths and skills and use those types of words in my summary statement. I think it helped me see myself in the next job and feel more confident that I did have what someone was looking for."
Meredith Ellison, Director, Education, AdvaMed

Chapter 3: Personal Branding for the Association Professional

Chapter

4 What Marketing Materials Should You Have?

The resume and cover letter are obvious, but there are other items that should also be included. Social media has become vital to the job search, which means you should have a keyword-rich, fully-branded profile for LinkedIn. Twitter and Facebook can also serve an important function in your job search. Additional materials include thank you letters, reference lists, and business cards.

Creating these documents is not as overwhelming as it may seem. Once you have the resume written, much of the information in it can be repurposed to create the other items.

Resumes

With so many ways to find out about someone online, you may be wondering if resumes are still relevant. They are! While positive information about you online can only help your image, resumes are still the core document in any career marketing campaign. Consider the following:

1. **Some employers require resumes as a matter of policy:** According to Shauna C. Bryce, Esq., of Bryce Legal Career Counsel, resumes might be used as documentation in the event a discrimination suit is brought against an organization.

2. **Resumes allow you to compete within Applicant Tracking Systems (ATS):** Organizations frequently use these to screen resúmes by computer. When hundreds of candidates apply for a position, these systems can help narrow the pool to a manageable number. Employers will search for keywords located in the resume. Those with the closest match will be reviewed by someone on staff.

3. **Resumes give decision-makers something to reference:** Hiring managers and human resources will likely review and discuss the resume several times during the process. It's also a standard format that can be used to compare candidates easily (unlike LinkedIn, a blog, or a website, where there will be more variation).

Even for those who realize that it's important to have a resume, they may not understand why they should give it much time and effort. However, with employers typically receiving more than100 resumes for each job opening, you can't afford to ignore this important document.

You may want to experiment with techniques to make your resume more visually appealing (text boxes, testimonials, etc.) While there are very few "rules" in resume writing, there are a few guidelines:

1. Make your heading the focal point of your resume.

2. Use a summary instead of an objective statement. Use this section to at least touch on your major qualifications.

3. Quantify your results whenever possible.

4. Keep your duties in one section and your accomplishments in another (note that the achievements in the sample are bulleted and bolded in the example below).

5. Write the resume targeted toward the position you want, not necessarily those you've held.

Jane Adams

123 Main Street • New York, New York 12312
(212) 555-5555 • janeadams@yahoo.com • linkedin.com/janeadams

DIRECTOR OF MARKETING
Making messaging matter!

Accomplished professional with 8 years of marketing experience in associations focused on animals. Proven success in driving membership increases through development and execution of integrated marketing campaigns. Results-driven leader skilled in creating innovative strategies to capture new markets. Core competencies:

Marketing Strategy	**Campaign Development**	**Brand Strategy**
Social Media Strategy	**New Business Development**	**Event Marketing**

PROFESSIONAL HISTORY

American Association of Veterinary Medicine, New York, New York
Nation's oldest association concentrated on furthering the veterinary profession; 100,000 members.
Director of Marketing, 2009–Present
Develop organization's overall marketing strategy and drive new opportunities for exposure. Direct marketing/communications staff of 10. Lead cross-functional teams in implementing integrated marketing campaigns to increase brand awareness.

- **Drove 17% increase in memberships of veterinarians with 10–15 years experience, due to targeted advertising campaign.**
- **Launched award-winning "What's Next?" campaign targeting mid-career veterinarians.**
- **Instrumental in 25% increase in conference attendance; created attention-getting campaign focused on new market.**

Continued...

Veterinary Association of Greater New York, New York, New York
The nation's largest regional association focused on expanding the veterinary profession; 19,000+ members.
Marketing Manager, 2007–2009
Assistant Marketing Manager, 2005–2007
Selected to lead staff of 6 in implementing marketing strategies to drive awareness of organization. Oversaw design and creation of all marketing collateral. Worked closely with membership department on campaign implementation.

- **Reduced annual printing costs 20% by switching vendors.**
- **Spearheaded expansion of social media, leading to a 10% reduction in annual marketing costs.**
- **Increased efficiency by automating portion of social media messages.**

Domestic Animal Association of Indiana, Indianapolis, Indiana
State association focused on educating pet store owners on the well-being of household animals; 300+ members.
Marketing Coordinator, 2003–2005
Supported staff of 9 in communications department. Created marketing collateral for distribution to retail pet stores. Assisted with development of direct mail campaigns and scheduled weekly e-blasts.

- **Increased monthly newsletter open rate 16% by administering survey to members and implementing suggested changes.**

EDUCATION AND TRAINING

Bachelor of Arts (BA) in Marketing
Purdue University, West Lafayette, Indiana 2003

Completed numerous professional development courses in branding and integrated marketing.

ADDITIONAL QUALIFICATIONS

Member of fundraising committee for Humane Society of America
Fluent in French

What do you look for on a resume?

"If they have previous NFP/assoc experience, even if it was just an internship or part-time job, it shows that they are interested in an altruistic position."
Katie Neisen Bromley, former Director, Grassroots and Congressional Advocacy, American Speech-Language-Hearing Association

"Resume experience matches the job requirements and it includes accomplishments, not just a list of responsibilities."
Beth Hampton, Chief Marketing Officer, The Optical Society

"Do they meet the minimum qualifications, is the resume written in a clear manner that clearly focuses on the individuals initiatives and successes, and finally is the resume free of errors. I am not looking for a laundry list of positions and responsibilities. I want to know what they have accomplished."
Jim Kendzel, Executive Director/CEO, American Society of Plumbing Engineers

"I look for experience (whether in my industry or not. I'm happy to take someone who is transferring their skills to a new industry) as a pre-screener to determine if I'll interview you. (As well as no typos or incorrect grammar in the cover letter and on the resume.)"
Betsi Roach, Executive Director, Legal Marketing Association

Cover Letters

There always seems to be debate about the importance of cover letters. Should you bother to include them? Does it need to be tailored to each job? Yes to both, with some very compelling evidence. According to a study done by Robert Half International, 86 percent of senior executives consider cover letters to be valuable. True, a full one-third said they never read them, but another third found them to be *more* important than the resume. The remaining third state they go back and read cover letters after skimming through the resume.

Even among the hiring managers who don't read cover letters, they may look negatively on the candidate who did not include one. It can appear that someone is lazy or doesn't pay attention to detail. In one scenario, they may use this as a deciding factor when trying to choose between two equally-qualified candidates.

So now you may understand the importance of the cover letter, but are completely overwhelmed at the thought of tailoring one for every job. It's actually easier and faster than you may be thinking. Notice that I said to "tailor" the cover letter for each job, not "write" a new one each time. The more jobs you apply to, the faster the "tweaking" will become. To start with a solid foundation, follow the steps below.

Writing a Cover Letter
Pre-steps:

1. Continue to communicate your brand by cutting and pasting the heading from your resume onto the top of your cover letter.
2. Click return and add the date.
3. Make three returns, and put the name, title, company, address, city and state, and zip code, each on separate lines.
4. Make one more hard return and type Dear (name):

The body:

1. **First paragraph:** Tell the reader where you had heard about the job, why you want to work there, and why you think you would be a good fit.
2. **Second paragraph:** Give highlights of your qualifications, and include a few examples. This can be in paragraph or bullet form.
3. **Third paragraph:** Show your interest in the position, and include a call to action. If you can find the contact information for a company, it's highly recommended you mention that you will be following up (but only if you're going to do it!). Thank the reader for their time and consideration.

Final steps:

1. Make a hard return, and type your closing (sincerely and respectfully yours work well).

2. Make three hard returns and type your name as it appears in the header (don't forget to sign it if you'll be printing out!).

3. Make a hard right and type "enclosure" or "attachment," since you'll likely be sending the resume along with it.

SAMPLE

Jane Adams
123 Main Street • New York, New York 12312
(212) 555-5555 • janeadams@yahoo.com • linkedin.com/janeadams

DIRECTOR OF MARKETING
Associations / Animals

July 17, 2011

Vincent Kucharski
Vice President
The Animal Society
123 Main Street
Chicago, IL 12312

Dear Mr. Kucharski:

With more than 8 years' experience developing and executing marketing campaigns for animal-focused associations, I am confident I can do the same for The Animal Society. Your *New York Times'* advertisement for a Director of Marketing and my background is an ideal match. My qualifications include a track record of driving membership increases, improving conference attendance, and reducing campaign costs.

Continued...

In my current position as Director of Marketing for the American Association of Veterinary Medicine, I lead the creation and execution of the marketing strategy and also develop new opportunities. Detailed in the attached resume, you will find ways I have added value to past organizations including:

- **Leading marketing plan resulting in the highest-ever attended conference.**
- **Decreasing costs up to 20% by evaluating and revising relationships with vendors.**
- **Elevating awareness of organization by creating innovative campaign targeting mid-career professionals.**

These proven qualifications would be an asset to a leading association such as The Animal Society. I look forward to speaking with you further and will call next week to arrange a mutually convenient time. Should you wish to contact me earlier, I can be reached at the telephone number and e-mail address provided above. Thank you for your time and consideration, and I look forward to our conversation.

Sincerely,

Jane Adams

Enclosure

Thank You Letters

Whether by e-mail or snail mail, handwritten or typed, a thank you note is a *must*—and the sooner it's sent, the better. There are many schools of thought on the best method, but my personal preference is to send a brief thank you e-mail that day, and a hard copy sent in the mail immediately. The e-mail should be sent to everyone you came in contact with, even if they did not interview you (for example, the receptionist).

Though some will disagree, I'm of the belief that the hard copy should be typed and not handwritten. Up to this point, everything else has been (or at least, should have been!) typed as well. Personally, I believe it gives a more professional image. The thank you letter can follow the basic "three-paragraph" format of the cover letter, with some obvious differences:

1. **First paragraph:** Thank the interviewer for their time.
2. **Second paragraph:** Reiterate *why* you are a fit for the position. Bring up examples discussed in the interview as well as how they're related to the job they're applying for.
3. **Third paragraph:** Show your enthusiasm for the job! It's a *must* to state that you are interested in the position.

It is perfectly acceptable to call and get contact information and correct spellings of names so that you can accurately send a thank you letter.

Jane Adams
123 Main Street • New York, New York 12312
(212) 555-5555 • janeadams@yahoo.com • linkedin.com/janeadams

DIRECTOR OF MARKETING
Associations / Animals

September 17, 2011

Vincent Kucharski
Vice President
The Animal Society
123 Main Street
Chicago, IL 12312

Dear Mr. Kucharski:

Thank you for taking the time to interview me for the director of marketing position. I enjoyed speaking with you, as well as learning about The Animal Society.

Meeting with you has further confirmed that I can fulfill your needs for a director of marketing. In addition to my passion for working with animals, my background in creating successful integrated marketing campaigns for associations can be leveraged to do the same for The Animal Society. I am also confident that my experience leading cross-functional teams would be an asset during the implementation of future campaigns.

Mr. Kucharski, I thank you again for your consideration. Serving as Director of Marketing for The Animal Society is the challenge that I have been seeking and I look forward to speaking with you again regarding this opportunity. Please feel free to contact me if I can provide you with additional information.

Sincerely,

Jane Adams

Reference Lists

In general, all the references you list should be professional. However, this does not mean supervisors only, though it helps to include at least one. You can also consider adding co-workers, direct reports, or vendors you interacted with. But use common sense. Don't list anyone who you wouldn't want to know that you're looking for a new job (such as your current supervisor). Provide as much contact information as you can find. Also, ask your references for permission before listing them. If nothing else, it's a courtesy, but you want to make sure they'll give you a flattering recommendation *before* you have a future employer call! Regarding design, the list should be branded and formatted to match the other written documents, such as in the following sample.

Jane Adams
123 Main Street • New York, New York 12312
(212) 555-5555 • janeadams@yahoo.com • linkedin.com/janeadams

DIRECTOR OF MARKETING
Associations / Animals

Sophie P. Bostick
Manager of Marketing
Veterinary Association of Greater New York
9275 Lily St.
New York, NY 12300
(212) 555-5380

Judith Chrisann
Brand Manager
Veterinary Association of Greater New York
9275 Lily St.
New York, NY 12300
(212) 555-5370

John Jordan
Director of Branding
Veterinary Association of Greater New York
9275 Lily St.
New York, NY 12300
(212) 555-5360

Michael F. Thomas
Senior Vice President of Marketing
American Association of Veterinary Medicine
1234 Broadway Ave.
New York, NY 12312
(212) 555-1212

Business Cards

If you don't have a business card, going to a networking event will be next to useless for you. This is how potential connections will remember you, contact you, and recommend you. How can they possibly do this without a physical reminder, particularly if they only spoke with you for 5 minutes?

The good thing is that getting business cards can be cheap, easy, and fast. Many local printers provide this service, but you can also create them at http://www.vistaprint.com or by printing them on your computer (though the quality may not be the same as with a professional company).

At a minimum, your business card should have your name, e-mail address and telephone number, and targeted job title. Ideally, it will also include a branded tagline, as well as other important information, which can include your LinkedIn profile, blog, or Twitter name.

SAMPLE

Jane Adams
janeadams@yahoo.com
212.555.5555
Director of Marketing
Specializing in associations focused on animals
Making messaging matter!
LinkedIn: linkedin.com/janeadams
Blog: http://www.janesmarketingblogging.com

Conclusion

Whichever document you're writing, and no matter what the job target, don't forget to *proofread!* Use spell check and then read through at least twice. It also doesn't hurt to have someone else take a look. Sometimes we get so used to our own work that our eyes skim right over errors!

Since many times a written document (whether a resume, cover letter, or LinkedIn profile) is your first introduction to someone, take the time to make sure yours are compelling, creative, and error-free.

5 Why Is Networking Important to Your Association Career?

Networking has become a popular buzzword, and with good reason—approximately 70 to 80 percent of people find jobs through word of mouth! Most employers, including associations, often try this method first because it's low cost, and referrals are already somewhat "pre-screened." According to Bill McHugh, Executive Director of the Chicago Roofing Contractors Association, when he has a position to fill, his first step is to reach out to his network in both the association world and the job's industry.

If, like many people, you're worried that you'll be bothering someone by talking to them about a job, don't be! Networking should lead to mutually beneficial relationships, so as long as you are willing to help others, you are on the right track. Plus, many organizations offer their employees a referral bonus, so you may be helping them even more than you know! Networking can help you in other ways. Promotions and other on-the-job opportunities often come from these types of professional relationships. Still, there are right ways and wrong ways to go about networking.

Ideally, you will have this network in place before you even need to look for work. As author Harvey McKay says, "dig your well before you're thirsty." Even if you haven't been actively working on building yours, you likely have the makings of a strong network from just from school and past jobs. However, as it can help you throughout your entire career, you can start growing yours at any time.

The Merriam-Webster dictionary defines a network as "a usually informally interconnected group or association of persons (as friends or professional colleagues)." That's pretty broad and can really mean anyone! While you can and should include people outside of your industry in your network (for example, there is no reason not to tell your best friend that you are looking for a job. Even if she is in a different field, she may know someone else in your industry), most of your dedicated networking time should be targeted as narrowly as possible. Targeted networking is covered in more detail in the section below.

How Else Can Networking Help You?

Networking is essential to career management, and not just when you're in active job search mode. While this is certainly the time to tap into your network, leveraging your connections can help you at any point in your career.

Getting Promoted

The same guidelines for searching for a job can apply when you are seeking a higher-level position at a new company. But, did you know you can also use networking to advance internally?

Consider this: You and an external candidate are vying for the same position. The other candidate is more qualified for the higher-level position than you are, and they actually held a similar role before. Still, you are not out of the running because the interviewer knows you personally. You've chatted in the break room several times, and she genuinely likes you. Plus, two of her direct reports have worked with you on a joint project, and pointed out to the hiring manager how you regularly went above and beyond. Based on the additional credibility that you got through interacting with fellow employees, the interviewer decides to take a chance on you and offers you the job.

Of course, it doesn't *always* work out that way, but you'd be surprised at how often it does. With significant numbers of new hires leaving (whether voluntarily or involuntarily) within the first six months, it makes sense that someone who comes highly recommended will have an edge over that someone else does not.

Internal networking can be easy in some ways (you are in the exact same place as your potential contacts, day after day!) but difficult in others (it can be hard to meet new people if you are not working on the same project, in the same department, etc.). To get to know others at different levels or outside of your department, attend as many "mixers" as possible. Whenever there is an all-employee meeting or party, volunteer committee, or even the chance to sit with new people in the cafeteria, take advantage of the opportunity.

Joint Ventures (JV)

When brainstorming new opportunities for your association, you may discover the need for a partnership with another organization. These JVs are more likely to happen (and more quickly!) when you have an internal connection. Even if they are not in the area you would be working with, chances are your contact can put you in touch with the right people.

When You Need to Hire

If you are actively hunting for a job, this might be the last thing on your mind right now. However, the time may come when you need talent, and the network of connections you have built is the first place to start looking.

If finding good employees is your main networking goal right now, follow the tips in the section below, but tailor it toward finding talent instead of a job.

Even if you are not in the position to hire for your department, recommending others for open jobs can have multiple benefits. First, you will be giving in the "give and take" of networking, and people will appreciate the reciprocal gesture. Second, you will be internally networking (see the promotions segment in this section), and your co-workers/managers will welcome the referral. Finally, if the person you recommended gets hired, there may be a referral bonus in it for you!

How Do I Find New Connections?

"Targeted networking" means deliberately seeking out people who may be able to help you in your career. These can be decision makers in your industry, colleagues who perform your same function, or prospective clients. Once you've identified who you need to come into contact with, the next step is getting connected to them. The list below will give you some ideas:

Meeting Online – This is the easiest way to start, especially when you are crunched for time. LinkedIn, Twitter, and Facebook are among the best ways to meet new contacts (see Chapter 6 for information on how use these methods), and stay in touch with those you already know.

E-lists offer another opportunity for meeting people. Yahoo and Google both have countless communities to choose from, based on your interests (just put Yahoo or Google + e-list into a search engine to get started). Look for those that focus on your industry or function. In addition, e-lists are often included as a benefit for association members.

Commenting on relevant blogs is also a good way to strike up a relationship. If the author ever responds to what you wrote (which they frequently do), use this opportunity to establish more of a connection. Consider taking the conversation off the blog and onto LinkedIn, e-mail, or even a telephone conversation. You can do the same when people comment on your blog (definitely something worth considering —see Chapter 3 for more information).

Getting involved in associations – Joining one or two associations related to your career goals, whether by function or mission, is the most highly-targeted way of networking. There are not many other places you can meet people so closely related to your career. There may be structured networking events, but there will definitely be volunteer and educational opportunities, both which are great ways to make new connections.

Expanding your existing network – Start with who you already know. If you are interested in working for the American Dental Association, but don't know anyone there, ask your existing contacts if they have any internal connections. Chances are good that either they do or someone they know does. If you do find a mutual connection, ask them to introduce you through a joint e-mail.

Reaching out directly – This is the most challenging method. If you just can't get introduced to the person you are interested in speaking with, you can reach out directly. The fact that you are making a cold call (or sending a cold e-mail!) means there is an additional barrier, but it doesn't mean connecting is impossible. Once you have determined who you need to talk to (e.g. director of fundraising, vice-president of finance, etc.), develop a strategy to get in touch with them. A few ideas include connecting with them through social media sites, calling the company directly, or sending them a targeted cover letter and resume.

A Networking Success Story

Carly Caminiti had been volunteering with smoke-free advocacy groups since high school. These led to internships and work opportunities during college. After moving to Spain, she wanted to get involved on a volunteer basis with similar associations. Through her U.S. contacts, she found the Spanish Society of Tobacco Control Specialists. Carly went in to talk about volunteer work, and left with a job! She worked on Spain's Smoke-Free Campaign for thirteen months, and the organization even paid for her master's degree in Tobacco Addiction. A lot of factors were at play, but Carly's wide network of industry contacts was instrumental in her getting a job in a new country.

Maintaining Your Network

It is not enough to meet new people. It is vital that you *stay* connected. The larger your network gets, the more challenging this is to do.

To make it more manageable, divide your contacts into two groups. For those you want to keep in touch with, but don't see an immediate need to talk regularly, follow up by LinkedIn. This is an easy way to keep your new contacts aware of what you are doing, without needing to put much effort into maintenance. You may want to drop them a personal note every so often, but the majority of your energy should be saved for the other group.

This is the group that you want to establish strong relationships with—the people who are in your target industry or those who are very well connected. It is still a good idea to connect on LinkedIn, but this is the group you want to give more personal attention to—phone calls, lunch dates, holiday cards. Nurture these contacts, as they are the "top-tier" of your network.

Maintaining these relationships actually does not need to take much time. Below are a few easy ways to keep in touch:

1. **Send information:** When you see an article, learn about a job lead, or hear about an event that may be of interest to one of your connections, pass it on to them. You will stay top of mind and also provide them with valuable information.

2. **Connect people:** This is one of the most important things you can do in networking, and it's fast! If there are people you feel could benefit from knowing each other, send a virtual introduction. Just cc both parties, give a brief introduction of each, and explain why you think they should connect.

3. **Send holiday cards:** If you are doing this anyway, it's easy to add a few more people to the list. For a twist, do what Wendy Terwelp, author of *Rock Your Network®*, recommends: Send cards on "weird" holidays such as Groundhog Day. You are practically guaranteed to stand out as the only person who contacted them for that holiday!

Maintaining your network is just as important as building your network. Give it the attention it deserves!

Conclusion

You have been networking naturally your whole life, so there aren't a lot of guidelines. The number one rule is to let others know you're always available to help. They may never take you up on it, but if you sincerely mean it, a new contact will be more likely to want to help you.

Also, be prepared to let others know how they can help you. If you are not sure, they can't do much even if they want to! Be clear on who you need to talk to, which associations you want to work for, and any other information you may need.

For an in-person event, don't forget business cards! If nothing else, they should at least have your name and contact information.

Make sure your LinkedIn profile is set up. Chances are whenever you meet someone new they will want to connect with you, or at the very least, view your profile.

This may seem like a lot of work, but with the majority of people finding their jobs through networking, making it a part of your career management plan should be high priority!

"My previous position with the New York Council of Nonprofits (NYCON) started as a Community Planner, a position that I found listed in our local paper. However, I knew many individuals in the community familiar with the association who supported my application and offered insight into the role NYCON played in the community."
Denise Harlow, CEO, NYSCAA, the NYS Community Action Association

---

6 Social Media in the Association Job Search

> *"I think the greatest means for an association or organization with the budget size similar to ours was/is by networking and through social media."*
> **Scott McCormick, Nonprofit CEO and President**

It's true! Associations *do* use social media to source for talent! Of course, they are not unique, as all associations want to keep costs down. However, this is even more likely for small associations with a limited budget. Not only is it cost-effective, it is also a way to reach thousands of interested candidates while pre-screening at the same time. Of course, online personas can be deceiving, but if your profile presents you in a positive light, it is one less obstacle you need to overcome prior to the interview.

Remember, social media should primarily be used for networking (it is often even referred to as social networking). The only real difference between online and in-person is the platform, and all of the same networking guidelines still apply. As a rule of thumb, if you wouldn't do something in person, don't do it online (such as asking someone you just met for a job). For more in-depth information, refer to Chapter 5 on networking.

Below are profiles of three of the most popular social networking sites, along with tips on how to use each of them for maximum effectiveness.

LinkedIn

If you have no other social media account, you *must* have LinkedIn. In some organizations, 70 percent of candidates are initially found through this site. The majority of recruiters locate candidates here, and even if they don't, they will still probably view your profile at some point. According to some employers, if you don't have a LinkedIn profile, you don't exist!

Still, I have had many clients who avoid putting up a profile because they are afraid it will signal to their bosses that they are looking for a new job. Though possible, this is extremely unlikely. LinkedIn has more than 100 million users and is growing every day. Many of these people are perfectly happy in their jobs and just want to make sure they are able to connect with others in their industry.

Now that you know the importance of having an account, it is also important to have a strong profile and proactively make new connections. It is not enough to set up a page and wait for people to contact you.

The Passive Part

First, write your profile toward the type of job you *want*, not necessarily the ones that you have had. Include plenty of keywords, which are typically the "hard" skills found in job descriptions—degrees, computer programs, and industry-specific terms. The more words that are included that match what a recruiter or hiring manager is looking for, the more likely you are to come up during a search.

Even though having someone find you is half the battle, you will still want to make sure your profile is high-quality, not just heavy on the keywords. As with the resume, emphasize what you can do, what you have done, and what your accomplishments are—quantifying and keeping them relevant to your job goal as much as possible.

A LinkedIn profile should not rehash the resume. While much of the information will be the same, it should not be repeated verbatim. Think of this as a cross between the cover letter and resume—adding highlights of your background, while at the same time introducing yourself in first person.

Don't forget to *complete* your profile. While in "edit" mode, there is a gauge that measures how far along you are. Those that are 100 percent complete are more likely to be viewed than those that are not. The two main things that keep people from finishing are the lack of a picture and three recommendations. Every effort should be made to include them.

Many LinkedIn users resist adding a picture. There are obvious reasons you should avoid including it on your resume (see Chapter 4 for more information on this), but social media is a different story.

People want to connect with people they like and trust, and including a picture is one important way to establish a relationship. Remember, it is still "social" networking, and you probably would not want to connect with someone new who didn't have a picture either!

The Active Part

Once your profile is complete, it is time to get active! Similar to most other social networking sites, there is an area where you can post your status. The main difference is that you do not need to do this every day. LinkedIn statuses have a longer shelf life, and you can typically wait seven to ten days before adding a new status. The information should be strictly professional, with an end goal of establishing yourself in your target field.

One way to start building your reputation is by participating in groups. Organizations across the world have groups that members and non-members alike can join. For example, if you join your college's alumni association, it will be displayed on your profile, immediately signaling to viewers that you are a member. From there, you can ask and answer questions, which is one of the best ways to get to know people in your areas of interest.

Though you can join up to 50 groups it helps to have a few where you regularly contribute and can build relationships with fellow members. Consider joining at least one national organization that serves association professionals, one that focuses on those in your geographic location (or desired location), and one for your job function (e.g. marketing, finance, or management). You will gain knowledge, make connections, and increase your credibility by participating in groups on LinkedIn. While it may seem overwhelming at first, this does not need to take more than ten minutes a day (or even every other day if you are using it in conjunction with other sites).

Twitter

Twitter is *not* just for teenagers and celebrities. Major organizations across the globe (including the White House!) are on Twitter, and unlike Facebook and LinkedIn, there is no barrier to you connecting with whomever you want. The secret to using it to get a job in an association is to develop and implement a targeted strategy.

First, as with LinkedIn, have a strong, keyword-rich profile. It is more challenging with Twitter, because you only have 160 characters for your bio. An easy way to sneak in extra words is to have your desired job title in the profile. For example, my Twitter handle is @*CharlotteWeeks*, but my name is listed as AssnExecCoach.

Remember how I said to be strategic when using Twitter to get a job in an association? Who you choose to follow (the term refers to how you connect with someone) is one of the most important ways you can put this into action. Make a list of all the associations you want to work for, all those that serve your industry (for example, the American Marketing Association if you are a marketing director), and former colleagues and classmates that work in similar fields. You can go to the search feature marked "Find People" and put the name in. When it comes up, click "follow." That's all there is to it!

Another great resource for finding people is http://www.Twellow.com. You can search by category (associations and organizations is a good place to start) or enter in keywords. For example, by putting in CAE, twenty-four pages of profiles come up, with a good number of them certified association executives.

An additional place to identify contacts is http://www.listorious.com. This site includes Twitter contact lists that have already been compiled. If you search for a term under lists (for example "healthcare associations"), you'll be able to follow numerous industry profiles in just one click. A definite time saver, it keeps you from having to go through each profile individually.

When you follow people, chances are that they, and other people with similar interests, will follow you back. Remember, the goal is not to get as many people as you possibly can to follow you. It is to develop a quality network with people you have something in common with. Note that as you start to follow people, you will see a bar on your front page which will suggest additional connections.

As with LinkedIn, setting up a profile and following people is not enough. Twitter is another networking platform, so you must engage people in order to start building relationships. With people commenting publicly, it is very easy to jump into a conversation. If you need somewhere to start, go to the main page of someone you are interested in getting to know better. See what they have said recently, and if you've got something to add, feel free to weigh in! Another easy way to start contributing is by posting articles of interest to your target industry. It also helps to add a brief comment with your thoughts.

Here are a few tips to help you get started:

Hash tags: These are referring to the # sign before a word. These allow your topic (for example #assn or #job) to be found by anyone searching for tweets on those words. Try it out yourself by putting a hashtag and term into the search box and join a conversation.

@: This symbol basically means "to." For example, if you want to address me specifically, you would put @*CharlotteWeeks* into the box titled "What's Happening?" and then add your message. It will be entered automatically when you reply to someone. Clicking the "@" icon on your page is like checking your e-mail inbox. You will see all the messages written to you and all the times you have been mentioned.

Retweets (RT): It is considered a great compliment when someone retweets you! Establish relationships with others by retweeting posts, articles, etc. that you find interesting. You can do this either by copying and pasting RT @name and the tweet (the method to use if you want to add a comment) or by clicking the "retweet" button on the bottom of the tweet. When someone retweets something you wrote, always say thank you!

Follow Friday/#FF/ff: Each Friday, people post the names of users they recommend others follow. Like a retweet, it is considered a great compliment and another way to build a relationship. When it happens to you, thank the person and consider mentioning them in your Follow Friday list. The hashtag and abbreviation is #ff.

Facebook

Facebook is typically thought of as a true social network, where only real-life friends interact. With 500 million people on the site (more than one-seventh of the entire world!), it seems to be a wasted opportunity if you ignore it in your job search.

Still, there are differences between Facebook and the "big two," LinkedIn and Twitter. First, it is primarily social, and should be treated as such. Connect with friends and family and feel free to let your personality come through (without oversharing—never a good idea on any online platform!).

Consider broadening your definition of "friends" (the term for connecting on Facebook). Former college, high school, and even grade school contacts may now be a good resource for you. Look up people you were friends with at another time (such as early in your career) that you have lost touch with. The wider your circle, the more opportunities will open up to you.

However, you need to let people know what it is you do and what you are looking for. This doesn't need to be in an annoying, blatant way. In fact, this is a great place to use Twitter as a guide. Every few days, mention something about your career—where you work, the type of work you do, or a class you are in. Make it conversational and people will naturally remember what you do. Another tactic is posting interesting articles related to your profession. Some Facebook friends may appreciate the topic, and people will be even more likely to remember what it is that you do. Stay even more top of mind and grow relationships by wishing your contacts a happy birthday (check the right hand corner daily to see who is celebrating a birthday).

While people are typically more guarded with accepting "friends" that they've never met, Facebook is an ideal place to connect with others' mutual acquaintances. I have seen it many, many times. One friend sees an interesting comment made by another friend on my page. It turns out they are in the same industry, so I introduce them via Facebook messaging. Before long, they have each added another contact to their network—all due to Facebook.

Facebook can also help you network in person. In the upper right hand corner (near birthdays) are event invitations. People frequently send these out to all of their Facebook friends so you will probably find a variety of options. When you see those that interest you, RSVP yes. That's all there is to it!

Conclusion

There are too many other social networks out there to name. It is more important to choose a few platforms and focus on interacting there. If you try and participate in more than a few, your efforts get diluted. Commit to those that you feel are most manageable (the three above are used by most job seekers and are recommended because of their size), and with just ten to fifteen minutes each day, you will meet more and more people who can help you with your career—without needing to leave the house!

"Many associations are also on Facebook which allow for posting of open positions to notify fans of availability. This makes it a great opportunity for recruiting from a pool already in tune with the organization."
Andre Blackman, Director, Digital Communications/New Media, American Heart Association

"We've recently begun posting on LinkedIn and I regularly post positions on Twitter and Facebook."
Kelly Siewert, HR Consultant, American Medical Association

"I connected with past colleagues through Facebook to schedule in-person networking meetings. This led to making contacts which resulted in me getting hired in my current position."
Linda Woody, Communications Manager, Association Headquarters

7 What Other Job Search Strategies Can You Use?

While networking is by far the most effective way to find a new position, it is still only one method (though it can enhance the others. A warm lead will help with any of the strategies below.).

In fact, when it comes to the job hunt, it's best to diversify and include various methods in your search. The key is to maximize your efforts by spending the most time and energy on the techniques that will yield greater results. Studies vary, but in general, this is the order of most to least effective strategies:

1. Networking
2. Applying to organizations that don't have an advertised opening
3. Recruiters
4. Job boards

Sending Your Resume to Companies without an Advertised Opening

The majority of my clients are shocked when I suggest this method, and even more so when they hear that it can lead to better results than applying to open advertisements online. How on earth can this be possible?

Consider the following situation. An association knows they have a position that needs to be filled. Whether they are waiting on budget approval, haven't gotten around to posting an advertisement, or are asking for referrals first (to avoid getting thousands of resumes), only a handful of people know about it.

During this period, a resume comes in for the very position about to be posted. The candidate seems to be a good fit, and they are brought in for an interview. The hiring manager and human resources representative can't believe their luck. They no longer have to deal with the headache of sourcing from scratch.

This happens more than you think. There could be a million reasons as to why a job hasn't been advertised yet, and at this point, you're only competing with yourself. Still, there are things you can do to increase the odds of making this method work for you.

1. **Develop a list of target associations:** Aim for at least twenty-five to fifty (though 100 to 200 is recommended) and go all out. Since you get to choose where you want to work, list your dream organizations. Consider what you would want in an association (location, size, focus, etc.) and add places that fit this profile to the list.

2. **Try and find contacts at each organization:** This is where your networking efforts will really come in handy. If there are places where you don't know anyone, do your best to get connected through your existing network or through LinkedIn (see chapters on networking and social media for more information).

3. **Send your cover letter and resume in the mail or by fax:** This will grab attention like nothing else! Because these methods are so rarely used, it is more likely they will be read than those where

an attachment needs to be opened in an already overloaded e-mail inbox. One human resources employee actually told me that he always reads faxed resumes because there are so few.

4. **Develop a systematic process for following up:** Keep a running list of when you sent a resume and cover letter, the date you called to follow up (I usually recommend three times, whether by telephone or e-mail), and any other notes. At a glance, you will always know where you are at with each organization, and since there will be so many balls in the air, you will naturally become focused on the process rather than on getting called back by a specific association.

Though this method can be time consuming, the results can be astounding. And with a significant number of employees leaving their positions within the first six months, companies are always on the lookout for good people. Since the job search is a numbers game, your odds can be increased considerably by having a larger number of associations on your list. However, there are certainly exceptions. One of my clients only got around to following this process with four organizations, and he ended up with two offers!

Recruiters

Recruiters can be an integral part of the job search. Statistically, 15 to 20 percent of people find positions through "headhunters," and for executives, this percentage is even higher.

There are still a lot of misconceptions about how recruiters work. They are hired by companies, not by candidates, and are sometimes the only channel to decision makers. Their goal is to find the one perfect person for an open position, which is typically a hard-to-fill job. They are then paid a placement fee after the candidate is hired.

So, how does someone go about getting in touch with recruiters? There are a few different methods I recommend to my clients.

1. **The Passive Method:** The next time a headhunter calls you about an open position, make a point of establishing a relationship. Even if you are not a fit for the job, treat them like a networking contact: Stay in touch on social media, send leads their way, follow up every few months by phone, etc. You will be top of mind when they do have a position that fits you, and they will be more likely to pass your name on to colleagues.

2. **The Active Method:** This is actually one of the fastest and easiest methods: using a recruiter distribution service. Your cover letter and resume will be blasted to headhunters across the country (who often source for companies in multiple geographic locations) hiring for associations in your area of interest as well as at your level. This can include hundreds or even thousands of firms. However, there are good and bad distribution services. Perform your due diligence and be sure to use a reputable company—one that doesn't "spam" and instead has a highly-targeted database of recruiters. It may cost more upfront, but it is likelier to bring you a higher return on your investment.

3. **The Active/Passive Hybrid Method:** This is a blend of both networking and the "passive" method. Conduct a targeted search to get in front of recruiters who source for associations and nonprofits, just as you would with hiring managers. Identify who you would like to talk to and get in touch with them, whether through LinkedIn, Twitter, introductions from personal contacts, or even cold-calling. From here, treat them as you would any other networking contact. Share leads, send articles, check in occasionally—anything to keep you in mind when a potential job opens up.

Any one of these tactics will increase your odds of getting a job through a recruiter, but for the best results, combine the three methods. It's not as overwhelming as it seems. Fifteen minutes a day is all you need.

Job Boards

Despite this method being the least effective way to get a job, it's actually the strategy people use more than anything else (which is the reason for its dismal track record—increased competition!) Still, people do continue to find jobs this way, or these boards wouldn't exist. How can you increase the chances that your resume will be chosen from the hundreds of applicants applying to open jobs online?

1. **Pack your resume with relevant keywords. (See Chapter 4 for more information.)**
2. **Mention a contact you have at the company.**
3. **Apply directly to a company's website.**
4. **Check out smaller "niche" boards that serve your industry.**

Despite these tips, it's recommended that you spend your time on more effective job search strategies and limit your online application hunt to one hour per day. Maximize your time even further by using a search aggregator like http://www.Indeed.com or http://www.SimplyHired.com. Both enable you to search multiple sites at once, and you can refine by location, salary, level, etc.

One exception to the above rule is Craigslist. Because of the low cost to post advertisements and the ability to narrowly choose a location, many associations have gone this route. However, since search aggregators don't pull jobs from Craigslist, you'll need to check their site separately.

Knowing where to look for open positions can be one of the biggest differences in searching for an association job, according to Cindy Simpson, CAE, Director of Programs and External Relations, Association for Women in Science. "It has been my experience that larger sites such as http://www.Monster.com are geared more towards for-profit entities. ASAE has a fabulous career site where many types of association jobs are listed. But be creative in your search. Google 'association jobs' and see what comes up!"

"Additionally," says Patricia Leeman, CAE Principal, Leeman Consulting Services, LLC, "CEO Update is worth the price for senior jobs." According to many of the people I interviewed, state associations (such as The Texas Society of Association Executives) and the Association Forum of Chicagoland, both list a wide range of jobs, and it is highly recommended you check them out during your search.

> *"We utilized as many inexpensive online posts first before going the route of engaging a recruiter."*
> **Scott McCormick, Nonprofit CEO and President**
>
> *"I've been very lucky. Three of my last four jobs I found online and the fourth was through personal contacts. I'm one of the rare stories who actually applied online and received a response, then an interview (or two) and then a job offer. A lot of time applying online can be like a black hole!"*
> **Betsi Roach, Executive Director, Legal Marketing Association**

Conclusion

There are exceptions to every rule, but these strategies are widely accepted best practices. Though each requires work, the payoff is well worth it. Just remember:

- Use all of the methods to uncover more leads and increase your odds of receiving an interview.

- Combine each strategy with networking.

- Follow up whenever possible.

- Though the job search can be discouraging, persevere, and you will succeed!

8 How Do You Successfully Interview at an Association?

> *"There have traditionally been two schools of thought in association management; hire a subject expert and teach association management or hire an association expert and teach the subject. Understanding that each organization's leadership reverts back to this fundamental decision and determines where they fall on the spectrum is likely one of the most important differences between associations and corporations."*
> **Melissa Heeke, Director of Communications and Marketing, National Chimney Sweep Guild**

The basics of interviewing at an association are the same as with any other organization. Still, there are some additional things you should be aware of that can give you an extra edge. This chapter outlines what you need to know to be as prepared as possible when interviewing for a position at an association.

Research the Organization

It helps to know as much as possible about the association you'll be interviewing with so that you can answer questions accordingly and sincerely express your interest.

It's easy to find information. At a minimum, the association's Internet site (especially the "About Us" page) will give you an overview of the basics including the organization's mission, history, and size. Hoover's, Dun & Bradstreet, and LinkedIn also have company information on their websites, and a Google search will likely yield even more details.

If you have contacts that work or have worked at the association, reach out to them for insider information. If you don't have any contacts, you may want to seek some out via LinkedIn or Twitter. If you're in the same group or have some other connecting factor, they may be more willing to speak with you.

Making Sure It's for You

The job interview is a two-way street! You'll save yourself a lot of trouble if you uncover any red flags *before* accepting a new position. Speaking with your contacts and researching the organization online will give you some information, but here are a few tips to dig a little deeper:

1. **Do a Google search, but go past the first few pages:** This is where you're more likely to find information that was not put out through the organization. The third party content you find may help you uncover things they don't want you to know.

2. **Check out** http://www.Glassdoor.com: This free website allows employees to anonymously post what they think about their organization. Opinions should be taken with a grain of salt, but they're worth reading.

3. **Observe:** When you go in for the interview, check out your surroundings. Do the employees seem happy? Are there a lot of empty offices (sign of a recent layoff)?

Prepare for the Position

The first step in preparing for position-specific questions is acquiring the job description. If it was advertised online, you can use the posting as a guide. If not, ask human resources to send it to you.

Once you have the qualifications in front of you, you can go about formulating answers for why you meet them. However, it's not necessary to come up with responses for every single line. Instead, look to the following:

1. **The top three requirements.** What themes jump out at you? What skill would be a deal-breaker if you didn't have it? By focusing on just a few main areas, you can come up with robust answers to what the interviewer most wants to know.

2. **The items closest to the top.** While there are certainly exceptions, in general the more important requirements are near the top. This is why you're more likely to have computer skills, specific degrees, etc. near the bottom. They're usually not essential to the core of the job.

3. **The qualifications you *don't* have.** Now is the time to determine what you'll say beforehand. Not only will you be able to downplay your lack of experience in this area, but you'll also feel more confident in the interview.

Formulate Answers

There are hundreds of questions you *might* be asked, and it's impossible to prepare for all of them ahead of time. The good news is, you don't really need to. Once you've determined the most important requirements of the job, you can come up with examples for each of them.

An easy formula to use is the "CAR" format: Challenge, Action, Result. Not only will this give you a blueprint to work from, but interviewers love hearing these types of responses. It lets them know that you've accomplished tasks related to the job (a good indication that you'll do the same for them if hired) while backing it up with examples.

Here's one example to give you an idea of how a CAR statement is put together:

CHALLENGE: Membership had been declining for years due to older members retiring and fewer people entering the profession.

ACTION: Designed a college recruiting program to promote the profession to students in relevant majors.

RESULT: Membership has been up 26 percent among 22 to 25 year-olds in the last two years.

Review the job description to determine the areas you should develop CAR stories for. It's recommended that you come up with ten to twenty CAR stories related to the required qualifications.

Practice Responses to Common Questions

There are questions that seem to pop up in just about every interview. Frequently asked by human resources, they include things such as "tell me about yourself" and "what are your greatest strengths?" Even when a question has a negative slant (such as "what's your biggest weakness?"), the "formula" I recommend is to keep each answer as relevant to the position at hand while remaining positive. Below are a couple examples:

Tell me about yourself. Many people are intimidated by this question because it's so broad. They don't know if the interviewer wants to hear about every job they've ever held or even information about their personal lives. Using the formula mentioned above, keep the response positive and related to the job to which you're applying.

For example, For Jane Adams, from Chapter 4 (a director of marketing seeking a position with The Animal Society), a response to this question might look like this: *"I graduated with a degree in marketing from Purdue and have been working in the field for the last eight years. Throughout that time, I've advanced from marketing coordinator to director of marketing, all while employed with associations focused on the well-being of animals. I've had considerable success in organizing membership campaigns, and just last year an initiative I led added 17% more members in the mid-career demographic. "*

What is your greatest strength? It's easy to keep this answer positive, but it should also be related to the job at hand. If you're applying to an accounting position that requires you to be on your own most of the time, saying "I'm outgoing and work well with people across all levels" isn't the best response. While it's a great skill, it doesn't mean much as far as the job is concerned. It's better to mention another skill you have that would be an asset to the position. For example, you could say you're highly organized, have an analytical mind, or possess strong problem solving abilities.

Frequently Asked Questions

There are hundreds of questions you "could" be asked, and it's useless trying to prepare for them all. However, it doesn't hurt to be aware of some of the most common questions (and what the employer really wants to know), which include:

1. **So, what do you know about our organization?** The interviewer wants to know you're interested in working for *them* and not in accepting any job that comes along. Share what you know and why it appeals to you.

2. **Why should I hire you?** They want to know why you're the best fit for the job. Be prepared to tie your skills and accomplishments to what the position requires.

3. **What questions do you have for me?** It's *vital* that you ask questions—otherwise, you run the risk of appearing uninterested. Prepare a few in advance. If they've been answered during the interview, ask the interviewer for more details on something that's already been discussed.

The Salary Question

Salary negotiations fall into a category of their own. The first thing to remember is to *never* be the one to ask the question. You run the risk of appearing that you only care about the job for the money.

Actually, you shouldn't answer this question either! Well, at least, not right away. Since the person who names a number first has the upper hand, it's recommended that you put off answering the question for as long as possible. The negotiation dance is one of the most difficult parts of the interview. People worry that by avoiding an answer that they'll appear difficult and not be considered further. Unfortunately, that is a risk, but the payoff can be huge! The key is to answer in a respectful manner. For example, "I'd love to hear more about the job and what it entails before I can give an accurate answer."

If you feel you must answer, it's best to give a range. Educate yourself on the going rate for your position and location by reviewing job ads, conducting informational interviews, and searching through http://www.payscale.com.

Handle Difficult Questions with Ease

Most people have at least one question they don't want to be asked! Typically, these include those related to getting fired, quitting a job after a short period of time, or having a gap on the resume. The "formula" for answering this type of question involves being honest, but not *too* honest. Tell the truth, but don't give too many details. It also helps to share what you have learned as a result. And as before, avoid saying anything negative about anyone else! For example:

Have you ever been fired?

Yes, once. I sent an inappropriate joke e-mail to a colleague of mine, which I now realize was a poor choice. Though he didn't mind, his supervisor had seen it since e-mails were monitored. I regret the decision, but have learned from it. I haven't ever sent a joke like that at work again and I never will.

Association Specific

Depending on the job you're applying for, previous association experience may not be necessary. Still, it's important to at least familiarize yourself with the industry, and of course, the organization itself. According to Sandra Giarde, CAE, Executive Director, California Association for the Education of Young Children, "The experience has to meet our needs. Folks with association experience either on a volunteer or staff level get extra attention." Here's what others who have done hiring for an association have to say:

"When interviewing at an association, I think it's critical to show a passion for what the association does and what it stands for. Knowing and believing in the mission and vision of an association is so important when trying to assimilate into the culture. I have found that most employees are really bound by our mission and it's what really motivates people to stay with us. We've got hundreds of long-term employees."
Kelly Siewert, HR Consultant, American Medical Association

"Today, if I was looking to hire someone, I would look for a background in customer service (because ultimately, in an association, you are dealing with members, who are your customers) and a candidate who can change gears at a moment's notice."
Lynn Sedlak, Executive Director, Connecticut Association of Optometrists

"Candidates need to understand that an association is also a business, just like a corporation. I've coined the phrase, 'we're not-for-profit, but we're not against it.' Simple homework like learning to create a business plan, understanding tax issues of not-for-profits, and concepts like inurement would help set candidates apart from the competition."
Jay Ahlman, Vice President, CPT and Physician Practice Solutions, American Medical Association

---

> *"Since associations are all about member service, I look for people who have a desire to please. I would rather have a smart, willing person with a customer service mentality and teach them the job, than an experienced person who doesn't have the right attitude or work ethic."*
> **Karen Peterson, CAE, SPHR, Executive Director, American Society of Hand Therapists**

Need to Know

How early should I arrive? Ten to twenty minutes is ideal. You want to allow enough time to fill out paperwork, get settled, etc. However, arriving more than twenty minutes early can make you appear desperate and the interviewer may resent that they feel they have to get started early.

What should I wear? There are so many options (especially for women!). As associations typically operate in a conservative environment, err on the side of caution and wear a business suit.

Can I take notes in the interview? Yes. You'll be able to better remember what you learned about the job and the organization (since the interview is for you as well!), and you'll appear interested in the job.

Close the Interview

Interview "best practices" include showing your enthusiasm for the job and asking about next steps as things are wrapping up. This serves the dual purpose of reminding the interviewer that you are interested in the position and it also gives you a timeline. There are a few ways to ask this question, including "when do you expect to make a decision?" and "what are the next steps?"

At the same time, consider bringing a "leave-behind," which is exactly what the name implies! It's something tangible that the employer can have to remember you by. Ideally, it will be another item that "sells you" and that they can read after you have left. For example, if you are interviewing for a marketing position, you may want to leave the interviewer with samples of campaigns you have worked on. Brainstorm ideas of what might work for you and your profession. A great product that I recommend to my clients regardless of their profession is WinTheView™. It's an interview preparation tool that you can design and print for presentation.

Should I send an e-mail, typed, or handwritten thank you note? There's not really a right or wrong answer; the most important part is that you send one as soon as possible! I usually recommend that a thank you e-mail is sent the same day, with a typed hard copy put in the mail the same day as well. Up until this point, everything has been typed and professional, so for consistency, I think it makes sense to do the same with the thank you letter.

Who should I send the thank you to? Everyone you met with, from the receptionist to the human resources representative to the hiring manager.

When should I follow up? Note that this says "when" and not "if." Following up after an interview is one of the most important things you can do. Use what the interviewer said as a cue. If they told you that they expect to make a decision in a week, it's acceptable to call back then to find out what the status is. If they say it'll be a few more days, call back then if you haven't heard anything. It's vital to check in, as it shows your interest in the position. Of course, use common sense. If you've been told "don't call us, we'll call you," respect their wishes.

Conclusion

Remember, the whole point of an interview is to demonstrate to the organization why you're the perfect fit for the job. Keep this at the forefront of your mind with every answer, and you can't go wrong!

9 Getting Promoted

Moving up in an association is a goal of many employees, but it can be a difficult one to accomplish. There is no road map, and as many "fell into" their careers in the first place, the same thing often happens with promotions. The good news is, there are many things you can do to improve your chances of getting tapped for a higher position.

Know Where You're Going

As the saying goes, if you don't know where you're going, how will you get there? Be clear on where you ultimately want to be (e.g. Vice President of Marketing at an association focused on XYZ), and determine what roles you need to aim for prior to that (e.g. Supervisor of Marketing, Manager of Marketing, then Director of Marketing) Once you've mapped out your ideal career path, it'll be easier to determine what's required to get you into your next role.

Many people who desire to get promoted run into the ultimate Catch-22: You need experience to be considered, but nobody will give you an opportunity to gain that experience. Still, it's not impossible, especially in an association. Before you go after more responsibility, it's vital to define what experience you need to acquire. Once you're clear on the position you want, review job descriptions and conduct informational interviews so you know exactly what qualifications are required. At this point, write down what experience you already have (you will be able to leverage this information in your resume and interview) and what you still need.

Consider, too, that you might even have more experience than you realize. For example, you may not have ever done fundraising or recruiting before, but you have held sales positions. See what other transferable skills you may already possess that you can leverage to convince your boss (or potential boss), that you are confident you can perform the required tasks.

Even if you need to acquire brand new skills, there are other ways they can be acquired. Many hiring managers in associations will consider someone who has learned on their own—whether through courses or volunteer work. In fact, these both have the added bonus of showing initiative. Plus, as a volunteer, you are demonstrating that you are committed to a cause, which is at the core of every associations' mission.

Still, getting the opportunity to pick up additional experience on the job is not impossible. This seems especially true with associations. Many of the people interviewed for this book shared the view that most people who work for associations need to wear multiple hats. When there's a task that needs to be done, everyone jumps in. This seems to be the case with most associations, but even more so with those on the smaller side.

This work may be handed to you, but if you want to use it as a stepping stone to your next position, you'll need to be strategic. For example, let's say you're a human resources assistant in an association and your goal is to become an in-house recruiter. Talk to the department decision maker and your boss about what opportunities may be available. Suggest things you can do to make things easier for everyone, while learning new skills that can benefit you. You may offer to screen resumes or handle the initial phone interviews. Assuming you get the go ahead for this, you can ask for more responsibility later on (such as picking up some in-person interviews). You'll actually be learning the job without holding it! Chances are, you'll be more likely to be considered when there is an opening or you can leverage this experience when you apply to another organization.

> *"My days most definitely do not consist of single tasks now. Today I worked on my society nominations, dealt with Ethics complaints, worked on planning a webinar dealing with healthcare reform, a summer workshop for Women Plastic Surgeons, in addition to dealing with follow up on two international programs that I manage. My days in the For Profit world were never that diverse!"*
> **Amy Papoccia, International and Specialty Relations Specialist, American Society of Plastic Surgeons**

Set Short Term Goals

Some things, like a master's degree or passing the CAE exam can take a while to accomplish. The sheer time commitment can discourage people from even getting started. While these may be in your master plan for your career, there are plenty of things you can do to start wherever it is you're at now.

Join relevant associations: This is a no-brainer. All you have to do is pay your membership fee and immediately you can say you're a "member of XYZ association." A few ideas include an "association for associations" (such as ASAE) as well as one related to your area of focus (such as the American Marketing Association if you're in marketing or the American Association of Medical Society Executives (AAMSE) if you're focused on a career in healthcare associations). While you always get out of an organization what you put into it, joining is the first step. From there, you can increase your knowledge and grow your network by becoming involved.

Attend continuing education sessions: These can include anything from an all-day in-person event to a thirty minute webinar. Decide what skills and subjects you need additional education on, and start learning! It's likely you'll have access to numerous free and low-cost educational opportunities as a benefit with your association membership. The best thing about getting training on your own is you don't need to wait for increased job responsibility to start picking up new qualifications that may be required in your next potential position.

Network within your industry: Recently the saying "It's not who you know, it's who knows you," has become popular—because it's true! You can be the perfect person for an open position, but if nobody knows it, what good does it do? An added bonus is that you may learn about new opportunities you'd never considered before (again, "falling into" something). Chapter 5 has in-depth information on how to make the most of targeted networking.

Set Long Term Goals

Once you know where you ultimately want to be in your career, you can identify the qualifications that may take you a while to acquire. As you advance in your career, you'll find these typically come down to three areas:

Experience: This is the area you have the least amount of control over. If a position requires 10+ years experience in an association, and you've only got five, there's no way to make the years magically appear. However, you can get yourself on the right track. If it's the same scenario and you're still at a corporation, start working on getting a job in an association immediately!

Master's Degree: More and more leadership position are requiring (or at least preferring) a master's degree. Not easy or quick, it's a significant time and financial investment. Still, if it's likely you'll need an advanced degree to meet your goals, think about when might be an ideal time for you to get started, and research schools with programs that fit your career path, schedule, and budget.

Certified Association Executive (CAE): The CAE is the designation awarded by the ASAE. The prestigious credential is awarded after a passing a rigorous exam. To even qualify to test, you need to meet the eligibility requirements which include completing 100 hours of approved professional development activities and a minimum number of years in the profession.

> *"The MPA is great. I believe I could take that knowledge and translate that into the public/government sector, or the private sector, and I definitely use the knowledge I gained almost every day in association work."*
> **Stacy Cheetham, Operations Manager, SmithBucklin**
>
> *"The CAE has helped by giving me the confidence and insight for how the work I do now could translate beyond industries to other associations."*
> **Jenifer Grady, Director, American Library Association-Allied Professional Association**
>
> *"Attend as many industry events as possible—in person, audio conferences, or webinars. Be prepared to participate and make valid contributions or ask questions of the presenters. As your name becomes more established, association executives will turn to you and think about you when they are looking to fill their next position."*
> **Cindy Simpson, CAE, Director of Programs and External Relations, Association for Women in Science**
>
> *"It can be hard for your manager to envision you in a different role. Show that you are up to the challenge by developing more efficient ways of doing things and handling procedures, offering solutions to problems, taking on more responsibility, and the like."*
> **Barbara Hollis, Senior Organization Development Consultant, American Medical Association**

Know How to Sell Yourself

If you are the perfect person for a position, but no one knows it, you need to learn how to showcase your talent! When you discover an opportunity you'd like to pursue, develop a game plan for selling the decision maker on you. Reference the chapters on personal branding, networking, marketing materials, and interviewing to get started.

Conclusion

Getting promoted isn't impossible, though it can certainly seem that way sometimes! Unfortunately, the reality is that some employers can't envision someone in a different role, no matter what their qualifications. It could also be that they are afraid to lose them in their current position. If you find that this is the case with your organization, it may be time to look somewhere that doesn't have preconceived ideas about you. Either way, persist and believe in yourself, and one day, you'll be hired by someone grateful to have found you!

10 Conclusion

Hopefully, you are convinced that a career in the association industry can be a richly rewarding experience. Though not for everyone, there are many that would never work anywhere else! It can be powerful knowing that by going into work each day, you're making the world a better place.

Using the skills you picked up in this book will lead to a job at an association, professional society, or membership organization. It's only the timeline that's hard to predict! Be patient, stay the course, and all your hard work will be rewarded.

Resources

Below are resources mentioned in the book along with others that can help professionals seeking an association career.

ORGANIZATIONS FOR ASSOCIATION PROFESSIONALS

AMC Institute
http://www.amcinstitute.org
Trade association serving association management companies.

American Association of Medical Society Executives
http://www.aamse.org/Home/index.asp
Professional association for medical society executives.

ASAE, The Center for Association Leadership
http://www.asaecenter.org
International membership organization that supports association professionals.

Canadian Society of Association Executives (CSAE)
http://www.csae.com
Organization for association executives in Canada.

The Federation of International Trade Associations (FITA)
http://www.fita.org
Organization for associations with an international mission.

REGIONAL SOCIETIES OF ASSOCIATION EXECUTIVES

Alabama Council of Association Executives
http://www.acaenet.org

Arkansas Society of Association Executives
http://www.arksae.net

Arizona Society of Association Executives
http://www.azsae.com

Association Executives of North Carolina
http://www.aencnet.org

Association Forum of Chicagoland
http://www.associationforum.org

California Society of Association Executives
http://www.calsae.org

Central Florida Society of Association Executives
http://www.cfase.org

Colorado Society of Association Executives
http://www.csaenet.org

Connecticut Society of Association Executives
http://www.csae.net

Dallas/Ft. Worth Society of Association Executives
http://www.dfwae.org

Delaware Valley Society of Association Executives
http://www.dvsae.net

Empire State Society of Association Executives
http://www.essae.org

Florida Society of Association Executives
http://www.fsae.org

Georgia Society of Association Executives
http://www.gsae.org

Greater Cleveland Society of Association Executives
http://www.gcsae.com

Idaho Society of Association Executives
http://www.isaeonline.org

Illinois Society of Association Executives
http://www.isae.com

Indiana Society of Association Executives
http://www.isae.org

Iowa Society of Association Executives
http://www.iowasae.org

Kansas City Society of Association Executives
http://www.kcsae.org

Kansas Society of Association Executives
http://www.accesskansas.org/ksae

Kentucky Society of Association Executives
http://www.ksae.com

Louisiana Society of Association Executives
http://www.lsae.org

Michigan Society of Association Executives
http://www.msae.org

Midwest Society of Association Executives
http://www.msae.com

Mississippi Society of Association Executives
http://www.msae-net.org

Missouri Society of Association Executives
http://www.msae.net

Montana Society of Association Executives
http://www.nvo.com/mtsae

Nebraska Society of Association Executives
http://www.nsae.org

Nevada Society of Association Executives
http://www.nsae.net

New England Society of Association Executives
http://www.nesae.org

New Jersey Society of Association Executives
http://www.njsae.org

New Mexico Society of Association Executives
http://www.nmsae.org

New York Society of Association Executives
http://www.nysaenet.org

Ohio Society of Association Executives
http://www.osae.org

Oklahoma Society of Association Executives
http://www.ok-osae.org

Oregon Society of Association Executives
http://www.osam.org

Pennsylvania Alliance for Association Advancement
http://www.paseae.org

Pittsburgh Society of Association Executives
http://www.psae.org

San Antonio Society of Association Executives
http://www.sasae.org

South Carolina Society of Association Executives
http://www.scsae.org

St. Louis Society of Association Executives
http://www.slsae.com

Tallahassee Society of Association Executives
http://www.tallysae.org

Tennessee Society of Association Executives
http://www.tnsae.org

Texas Society of Association Executives
http://www.tsae.org

Utah Society of Association Executives
http://www.usaeinfo.com

Virginia Society of Association Executives
http://www.vsae.org

Washington Society of Association Executives
http://www.wsaenet.org

West Virginia Society of Association Executives
http://www.wvsae.org

Wisconsin Society of Association Executives
http://www.wsae.org

JOB BOARDS

Associationjobs.org
http://www.associationjobs.org
Source for open association positions at all levels.

CareerHQ
http://www.careerhq.org
ASAE's job board, with association positions listed throughout the country.

Craigslist
http://www.craigslist.com
Classified advertisements by city.

Indeed
http://www.indeed.co.in
Aggregator pulling job advertisements from thousands of sites.

SimplyHired
http://www.simplyhired.co.in
Aggregator pulling job advertisements from thousands of sites.

BOOKS

I'm on LinkedIn—Now What??? by Jason Alba
Resource for maximizing LinkedIn features for career management.

I'm on Facebook—Now What??? by Jason Alba
Guide for using Facebook as a networking tool.

Rock Your Network® by Wendy Terwelp
Practical guide to growing your network.

Sway Factor: The Art of Networking in the Digital Age by Sima Dahl
Learn how to use social networks to build your personal brand. *To be released.*

The Twitter Job Search Guide by Susan Britton Whitcomb, Chandlee Bryan, and Deb Dib
Comprehensive resource on using Twitter to search for a job.

MISCELLANEOUS RESOURCES

Associations Now Magazine
Magazine included with membership to ASAE. Also available by subscription.

Association *TRENDS*
http://www.associationtrends.com
Online publication providing industry news to senior association executives.

CEO UPDATE
http://www.ceoupdate.com
Print publication (with additional material posted online) for association executives. Also includes postings for senior-level association positions.

FORUM

InTimeTV
http://www.intimetv.com
Internet television producing talk shows for professionals. Includes the show, "Association Exec's."

JIBBER JOBBER
http://www.jibberjobber.com
Online tool to help you manage your network.

Listorious
http://listorious.com
Identify and follow already-created Twitter lists.

The National Resume Writers' Association
http://www.thenrwa.com
Member-driven association for writers of career documents. Includes database to choose writer based on location and specialty.

Twellow
http://www.twellow.com
Directory of public twitter accounts, searchable by various criteria.

WinTheView.com
http://www.wintheview.com
Tool for interview preparation and presentation.

SOCIAL MEDIA

Linkedin
http://www.linkedin.com
Website focused on connecting professionals. Currently has more than 100 million users.

Twitter
http://twitter.com
Social networking site for connecting socially and professionally.

Facebook
http://www.facebook.com
Website used primarily for developing social contacts.

RESEARCH SITES

Glassdoor.com
http://www.glassdoor.com
Website with insider information posted anonymously by employees.

HOOVERS
http://www.hoovers.com
Provides business information about companies and industries.

The Occupational Outlook Handbook
http://www.bls.gov/oco
Released by the U.S. Department of Labor; provides overview of hundreds of jobs.

O*NET Online
http://www.onetonline.org
Comprehensive source of information on occupations; developed under sponsorship of the U.S. Department of Labor and Training Administration.

WEDDLE's
http://www.weddles.com
Website which includes a listing of associations by category.

About the Author

Charlotte Weeks is a career coach and resume writer specializing in helping association executives to find their passion and land at the top. Prior to launching Weeks Career Services, Inc. (http://www.weekscareerservices.com), she was employed in an association, and currently serves as president of The National Resume Writers' Association.

Active in both the careers and association industries, Charlotte is a member of several organizations, including ASAE and The Association Forum of Chicagoland. She has served as an industry expert for various media outlets including The Wall Street Journal, CareerBuilder, and NBC-Chicago.

Avid travellers, Charlotte and her husband Mike call Chicago their home base.

Other Happy About® Books

Purchase these books at Happy About http://happyabout.com or at other online and physical bookstores.

I'M IN A JOB SEARCH
Now What???

KRISTEN JACOWAY
FOREWORD BY JASON ALBA
HappyAbout info

I'm in a Job Search—
Now What???

The book provides 100+ resources and tips to guide you through the job searching process to help you stand apart from your competition.

Paperback $19.95
eBook $14.95

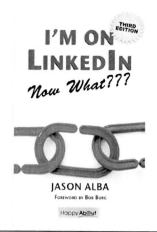

I'M ON
LINKEDIN
Now What???
THIRD EDITION

JASON ALBA
FOREWORD BY BOB BURG
HappyAbout

I'm on LinkedIn—
Now What???

This LinkedIn book is designed to help you get the most out of LinkedIn, which has become the most popular business networking site. It is one of "the big three" in the social networking space, along with Facebook and Twitter.

Paperback $19.95
eBook $14.95

STORYTELLING ABOUT
YOUR BRAND
Online & Offline

BERNADETTE MARTIN
FOREWORD BY WILLIAM ARRUDA
AFTERWORD BY JASON ALBA

Happy About

Storytelling about Your Brand Online & Offline

Using this book, professionals and executives of all types, entrepreneurs, consultants, musicians, academics and students will undergo a "personal branding process."

Paperback $22.95
eBook $16.95

Social Media Success!

This book is a launch pad for successful social media engagement. It shows how to identify the right networks, find the influencers, the people you want to talk to and which tools will work the best for you.

Paperback $19.95
eBook $14.95

More Praise for I'm on LinkedIn—Now What???

"This book may put an end to the 'accidental association professional.' Concise and informative, Weeks leads the reader through a practical process of how to land an association career."
Julie Stelter, President, Walden Group

"I Want to Work in an Association—Now What??? is a useful reference when beginning your career, and provides key insight in obtaining a position within an association. The book highlights the importance of networking, branding yourself, and includes helpful links and resources. The author shares testimonials from association executives that demonstrate how association management is a true profession and career. From my past experience of managing an association job board, no two career paths of association executives are ever the same, and this book embraces that fact!"
Marta Hayes, Managing Director, Hayes Project Services

"I Want to Work in an Association—Now What??? is a true gift to anyone who is even remotely interested in working for an association. Weeks has done a brilliant job of crystalizing a wealth of valuable, must-have information into a concise, interesting, and informative read."
Robyn Feldberg, Executive Career Coach/Resume Writer,
http://www.abundantsuccesscoach.com

"Full of practical advice, I Want to Work in an Association—Now What??? is the essential guide to the many fulfilling and exciting career opportunities within associations. From personal branding to the interview process, networking to career growth, this book is a must-read for the job candidate looking to set himself apart."
Liz Cies, Public Relations Coordinator, Association Headquarters, Inc.

"Association management is a richly rewarding profession that too few know about. Charlotte Weeks has produced a helpful guide for learning about and succeeding in the association management. I wish I had this when I got started!"
Oliver P. Yandle, Esq., CAE, Executive Vice President, Commercial Law League of America

"As someone who speaks to professionals interested in a career in association management on a very regular basis, I was delighted to read Charlotte Weeks' book. It is an easy read with a good overview of how associations are unique and step-by-step instructions and resources for beginning your search in this great industry."
Christie A. Tarantino, CAE, President & CEO, Association Forum of Chicagoland

"From resume writing and follow up to social media search strategies, now there is finally a great handbook for job seekers interested in targeting professional associations for employment and career mobility."
Laura DeCarlo, president of the global association, Career Directors International

"In this book Charlotte Weeks builds the case for seeking employment within associations, as well as providing actionable and specific advice to potential job hunters. Clearly and concisely written, this book will certainly prove to be a valuable resource to those interested in pursuing an association-related career path."
Andy Bostick, Senior Researcher, American Hospital Association

"College students in search of a career that combines passion with practicality will jump at I Want to Work in an Association—Now What???—a step by step guide to jobs with professional associations, membership organizations, or societies. This is the first book out there that showcases the association marketplace: what the jobs are, where they are, how to successfully land a job, and how to climb the association career ladder. No college career library should be without it."
Marianne Green, Assistant Director, Career Services, University of Delaware

"Solid career advice, insider secrets, and specific steps on what it really takes to land your dream job in an association!"
Susan Whitcomb, author of seven careers books including Resume Magic, and CEO of the career coach training organization, TheAcademies.com

"I Want to Work in an Association—Now What??? is a great book for someone who may be interested in association work or just landed a job with one because the association world is new territory for most. With two and half years of association work experience myself, I too found this information beneficial and great as I contemplate my next steps in my career."
Katie Masterson, Senior Education Program Manager, American Society of Interior Designers

"Looking for a job in the association world is tough work, especially today. This is not your parents' job market. You are competing with many others for the same position; the key is how you separate yourself from the crowd by being more practical and innovative in the search. Charlotte Weeks describes just that in her book, I want to Work in an Association—Now What??? She's provided the real-world tools to maximize job hunting results. Great job, Charlotte, and good job hunting readers!"
Mick Weltman, President, Weltman Consulting,
http://www.weltmanconsulting.com

"This focused, easy-to-read guide is a great primer for job hunters of all kinds. While addressing specific aspects of trade and professional associations, the tips can be applied to just about any employment opportunity."
David M. Patt, CAE, Association Executive Management

"A resource that finally lays out the ins and outs of getting hired to the association of your choice."
Jeanette Brown, MBA, Marketing Strategy Manager, Informz, Inc.

"Working in an association is an extremely rewarding career — you help others by working towards the mission of the association and you can benefit from personal fulfillment and satisfaction. Charlotte has explained the ins and outs of how to find that wonderful career that is waiting for you!"
Linda S. Chreno, CAE, IOM, Association Connector, San Leandro, CA

CPSIA information can be obtained at www.ICGtesting.com
Printed in the USA
241555LV00002B/7/P